AMERICAN FREAK SHOW

THE COMPLETELY FABRICATED STORIES OF OUR NEW NATIONAL TREASURES

WILLIE GEIST

HYPERION
NEW YORK

Copyright © 2010 William R. Geist

Library of Congress Cataloging-in-Publication Data has been applied for.

ISBN 978-1-4013-2394-3

Hyperion books are available for special promotions and premiums. For details contact the HarperCollins Special Markets Department in the New York office at 212-207-7528, fax 212-207-7222, or e-mail spsales@harpercollins.com.

Design by Renato Stanisic

FIRST EDITION

10 9 8 7 6 5 4 3 2 1

For Mom and Dad,
who taught me that the freaks are
always more interesting

ACKNOWLEDGMENTS

★

I've always found the term *Acknowledgments* a little weak for a book's thank-you list. An "acknowledgment" is quite literally the recognition that someone or something exists. It's important to me that you know the following people exist in human form, but more importantly that I appreciate their support and guidance. In fact, let's go with *Appreciations*.

First and foremost, to my wife and most trusted editor, Christina. She's been helping me with my homework since Mr. Kaplan's sixth-grade English class. No chapter was good enough until she laughed out loud.

To my beautiful babies, Lucie and George, for growing up in a city whose nursery school tuitions put the Ivy League to shame. I had no choice but to take a second job.

To my sister Libby, the funniest chick I know. She's endured a lifetime of my material.

To Tom Connor, my literary agent and longtime family friend, for convincing me that writing a book while hosting a daily early-morning television show and raising two small, helpless children was a good idea. I wish he'd been more clear that you actually have to *write* the book after signing the deal. I'll read the fine print more closely next time.

To Gretchen Young, the superstar editor at Hyperion, for giving me complete freedom but stepping in to save me from myself when necessary.

To Elizabeth Sabo, Ellen Archer, Elisabeth Dyssegaard, Marie Coolman, and Christine Ragasa at Hyperion. And to Will Balliett, the man who brought me in and wisely got out before I brought the entire publishing house to its knees.

To my extended family, the Lewises. Especially "The Uncles"—Herb, Mike, and Bert—whose performances around the Christmas dinner table scarred me for life. I'm so glad they did.

To my friends Joe and Mika, for sucking me into the fantastic ongoing freak show that is *Morning Joe.*

And finally, to Jonas Salk for finding the polio vaccine. Just one less thing I have to worry about. Nice work, man.

CONTENTS

★

CONTENTS

18

The People of Heaven v. John Edwards

19

Snooki and the Salahis:
The 15 Minutes Hall of Fame

Index

INTRODUCTION

★

I was sitting on the set of *Morning Joe* one day talking to my friend and cohost Mike Barnicle during a commercial break when a loud, confident voice shot across the studio, interrupting our conversation: "Morning, fellas! I'm innocent of all charges!" You have to understand that very few of our guests on the show include a legal plea in their personal introduction, so it didn't take long to figure out who had arrived. Blago was in the building. We'd been expecting him.

Former Illinois governor Rod Blagojevich was there to promote a book, but watching him move across the room, you would have thought he was running for third-floor fire warden in our building. He shook the hand of just about every member of our crew (and those of some confused foreign tourists who wondered why a strange, aggressively enthusiastic man with odd hair was telling them he was innocent of an unspecified crime—was he part of their NBC tour?). After signing a couple of unsolicited autographs, Blago leapt onto the set and launched into what sounded like the dry run of an opening statement for his pending trial.

He warned us that a political smear campaign was under way in "the great state of Illinois." But this, he assured us, wasn't about one man and his reputation. It was about a perversion of the American justice system. It was about an audacious disregard for the basic principles of fairness, right there in the Land of Lincoln. Above all, though, it was about his new book, *The Governor*, available wherever fine books are sold.

In less than 60 seconds, Blago's performance already had exceeded our lofty expectations. We at *Morning Joe* had been steadfast, unapologetic Blago supporters, eschewing the disrespectful term *disgraced* that the rest of the media always seemed to use to preface his gubernatorial title. We preferred "*persecuted* former governor." Christlike persecution was a theme Blagojevich had been pushing, and we were happy to indulge the narrative of "Blago as martyred religious figure."

During our interview, Blagojevich explained that the Illinois state legislature removed him from office in something of a bloodless coup, reversing the will of the people simply because he was trying just a little too hard to bring health care to sweet little children whose families could not afford it. In Blago's telling, his only crime was having a heart too big. For that, he lost his job. We did not ask him to elaborate on this point—details would have ruined the poetry of his argument.

After the interview, during which Blago confessed only to having used some foul language on an FBI wiretap (who among us has not?), I mentioned to the former governor that my mother is from Chicago and my dad from downstate Champaign, Illinois. My father, who covered the city for the *Chicago Tribune* in the 1970s, had recently come to appreciate Blagojevich's bullshit artistry and charming, old school Chicago (alleged) corruption. To my surprise, Blago suggested we give my dad a call. At home. Right then. "Now?" I asked. Blago assured me he was quite serious. He wanted to talk to my father.

I dutifully whipped out my BlackBerry and called my parents' home number. I wasn't quite sure what Blago had in mind, but it really didn't matter. When you're offered an audience with Blago, you don't ask a lot of questions. He's papal in that regard.

My mom answered. "Mom, put Dad on the phone. It's important," I said sternly. It *was* important. She sensed the urgency in my voice and summoned my dad to the telephone. I announced to my old man that the former governor of the great state of Illinois would like a word with him. I couldn't say why. Not because it was confidential, but because I genuinely could not provide a reason why the governor wanted to talk to my father. I handed the phone to Blago, stepped back, and watched a master at work. Some say Barack Obama is the greatest orator of our time. With due respect, I say he isn't even the best in Chicago.

Over the next two minutes, Blago performed an uninter-
rupted monologue that included several declarations of innocence, repeated promises not to let my father down, sincere
thanks for his ongoing support during these difficult times, a
solemn pledge to keep fighting for my dad and for *all* the people
of Illinois who put him in the office to which he intended to
return soon, and, naturally, high hopes that this would be, at
long last, the year for those Cubbies.

After listening to that speech, how could my dad possibly
break the news to Blago that he hasn't lived in Illinois since
1980? We just went with it. It seemed unlikely that my father
would be called from New York City back to Cook County
for jury duty on the Blagojevich trial, but my dad and I sure as
hell weren't going to get between a man and his mission to
personally heal the wounds of his state, one potential juror at
a time.

Blago eventually said good-bye to my father and handed the
phone back to me. He then asked for a pen to sign one more
autograph, he posed for a couple of photographs, he proclaimed
his innocence to an unwitting member of the cleaning staff,
and then, just like that, he was gone. Our brush with Blago was
over. He belonged to the world again, but for that brief, shining
moment he was ours.

My dad had always held up the "Vote early, vote often"
Mayor Daley as the gold standard for Chicago political characters, but he conceded to me after that phone call, "Okay, you're
right: Blago is the best." It was an oddly poignant father-son
moment. For better or worse, my dad has passed down to me

an attraction to the American Freak Show. And there I was, rubbing elbows with one of the great freaks of our time. I mean that purely as a compliment, by the way.

My father, who has made a successful career of following strange people around the country and telling their stories, taught me not to waste time protesting the self-inflated showmen and bloviating bullshitters who populate our culture. It's more fun to marvel at them, to appreciate them, to be grateful for them, and to mock them relentlessly. I was taught to applaud audacity like that shown by an impeached Illinois governor who once said he could relate to "Mandela, Dr. King, and Gandhi." Come on, that's great shit. Self-righteously calling out Blago for being a cartoonish charlatan is like declaring loudly that cheeseburgers are bad for you. Of course they are. That's not the point. They're goddamn delicious. And the bigger, the better.

So I say, let others judge the (alleged) sins of Rod Blagojevich. I salute a man who proudly represents the new instant American celebrity—thrusting himself into our lives out of nowhere with an act of human frailty (or, you know, criminal wrongdoing) and then redeeming himself through the magic of reality television. Like most of the characters in this book, Blago came without warning, sent from the pop culture gods to entertain us briefly before inevitably evaporating into the ether, leaving behind only a thinly sourced Wikipedia page full of memories.

The stories you're about to read are made up, but the people are all quite real (except for John Edwards—it turns out he's

actually one of those security dummies people put in their passenger seats so they can ride in the HOV lane). You know the
characters well, even if you've tried to avoid them. They are
criminals and creeps, hypocrites and heathens, gluttons and
Gooselins. Yes, they are freaks, but they're *our* freaks. So pull
up a seat and enjoy the show.

1

President Palin:
The Inauguration Address

★

TAMPA, January 21, 2013—Determined to reinforce the "Washington outsider" image that swept her into office two months ago, President Sarah Palin held her inauguration ceremony tonight at the Ice Palace arena in Tampa, Florida, during a live episode of World Wrestling Entertainment's *Monday Night Raw*. Bucking inaugural tradition, President Palin was sworn in as the nation's forty-fifth president immediately following the highly anticipated grudge match between former tag-team partners John Cena and the Undertaker. President Palin precipitated the end of that match by striking Mr. Cena across the back with a metal folding chair, drawing cheers from the supporters gathered to hear her speech. Presidential historian Doris Kearns Goodwin confirmed to the Associated Press that Mrs. Palin is the first president to have participated in a professional wrestling match on the day of her inauguration.

The oath of office was administered by Judge Larry Joe Doherty, host of the popular syndicated show *Texas Justice*. In a departure from protocol that stunned constitutional scholars, Palin refused to take the oath from the Chief Justice of the United States Supreme Court. Palin called Chief Justice John Roberts "a good man," but "another Beltway insider who has grown out of touch with Real America." Palin added, without prompting, "I sure as heck wasn't gonna have that liberal Spanish lady from New York City give the oath. Might as well just hand the country over to the illegals at that point." Without having reviewed the complete historical record, Kearns Goodwin speculated that this evening's inauguration was the first presided over by the host of a syndicated television program (note: Judge Reinhold was offered the honor by President George W. Bush, but declined).

Hitting the familiar broad themes from her successful campaign, President Palin's remarks were notably brief by historical standards. Her aides cited pressure from WWE officials to leave time in the broadcast for a planned "Legends Rematch" between Sgt. Slaughter and the Iron Sheik. A senior staffer, speaking on the condition of anonymity because he generally did not wish to be associated with Mrs. Palin, said the president-elect agreed to curtail her address because "she knew America wanted to see an Iranian terrorist wrestler get his butt whooped by a patriotic American." According to the source, Palin also said she remembered from her friend Cindy's "super-lame" rehearsal dinner how annoying a long speech can be.

The following is a copy of President Sarah Palin's inauguration address, as prepared by Palin herself:

> *Good evening, my fellow Americans!* (pause for standing ovation and "Sarah! Sarah!" chant) *I am so proud to be standing here as your President of America!* (pause for even bigger cheers) *Hell yeah! Welcome to Inauguration 2013, brought to you exclusively by the people at Arctic Cat Snowmobiles, who invite you to "Share Our Passion."* (pause and let animated Arctic Cat run across the bottom of the screen so we get the free sleds they offered in exchange for the inauguration shout-out) *Before we get started here, I want to point out that Todd has a card table set up out on the concourse to sell his new DVD* Wipeout! The First Dude's Most Awesome Snowmachine Wrecks Ever! *Pick one up on your way out, and not just because Todd is a majorly hunky guy!* (wink) *Seriously, the wrecks are awesome. People die in some of them, and, ya know, life is so precious and whatnot.*
>
> *I want to begin this evening by thanking my tag-team partner during this long campaign fight. Please welcome my running mate and dear friend, the brand-spankin'-new vice president of YOUR United States of America, "Nature Boy" Ric Flair!* (huge cheer) *His enthusiasm and belief in America's fundamental greatness are so appreciated by me.*

And how cool was that clothesline move he pulled on Joe Biden during the debate?! (pause for "Nature Boy" to do that awesome "Whooooooooo!" thing he does)

Ya know, they told me I was crazy to hold my inauguration on WWE's Monday Night Raw. *They said, "Sarah, this just isn't the way things are done. . . . Ya gotta do it on Capitol Hill in Washington, D.C."* (pause for boos— everyone hates D.C. and the people who live/work there, except for Michelle Bachmann—she's a doll) *And I'm sittin' here thinkin' to myself, "Is this the same Capitol Hill where nothin's been gettin' done for the past few hundred years or so, except when Reagan was there?"* (pause for wild cheering) *"Is this the same Washington, D.C., that's been trying to tell the rest of us what to do for the last 4 years? The same Washington, D.C., that's force-feeding us health care we never asked for?"* (loud boos) *Ya know what I told 'em? "Thanks, but no thanks on that speech in Washington. I'm gonna go share this night with my friends down in Tampa and on TV screens across this great nation of ours."* (wild cheers)

So here we are at the Ice Palace, home of the 2004 Stanley Cup champion Tampa Bay Lightning! (big cheer— people relate me to hockey and remember my killer zinger at the '08 convention about pit bulls and hockey moms) *The only thing sweeter than winnin' the presidency is winnin' that Cup! Am I right, Tampa?!* (more cheers)

Listen, I know you're waiting to see Sgt. Slaughter come out of retirement to open a can of you-know-what on the Iron Sheik, a terrorist wrestler from Iran (loud boos—I'd take down that dirty terrorist myself if they'd let me), *so I won't keep ya here long. Plus, I don't want to make this one of those long snoozefests like the last guy used to give us. Dear Lord, Hussein Obama, my kids are gonna be grown up by the time ya finish talkin' about all your inside-the-Beltway gobbledygook!* (laughing and cheers—people are fed up with this Indonesian guy, Obama) *We get it: you went to Harvard. You know a lot of stuff. Congratulations. Now stop interrupting my* Supernanny *show with these dang prime-time speeches!*

Thank God those days are over, huh? Before I begin, I want to first thank Sgt. Slaughter for his brave service to this country (pause for cheers—I assume he served in Vietnam . . . he's wearin' a camouflage leotard) *and I look forward to him wiping the floor with this foreigner whose country continues to hide its nuclear ambitions from the world.* (pause for chants of "Towelhead!" as prompted on the JumboTron) *I don't know what the last guy told ya, Mr. Sheik, but I'm here to tell ya that America's days of appeasement and not attacking you with our full military might are officially over!* (crowd erupts, waves flags, chants U-S-A!)

And that being the theme of my inauguration speech here—American greatness and an unwillingness to apologize for it, as others have been so eager to do. There are those who have said America is diminished by a weak economy and a foreign policy that rubs some the wrong way. Well, I've got one thing to say about that: If it rubs ya the wrong way, you're free to leave . . . the world! Leave the world if you don't like it!

That's right: get off the Earth planet! (pause for wild cheers—people do NOT like foreigners) *How's that for a foreign policy, China?! The last time I checked, Ronald Reagan beat the Communists a long time ago. Oh, and get me an egg roll while you're up!* (more cheers—people really seem to love egg rolls, although I don't see their appeal . . . where's the beef?!) *I'll be sure to get right back to ya with that trillion bucks we owe ya, by the way . . . not!* (laughter and cheers—people like having their credit card debts forgiven) *America doesn't owe anybody anything, my little Oriental friends.*

So on the foreign front, no apologies, and back here domestically, just believing that hard-working Americans can get the job done. I intend to put our great citizens back to work and remind the world that America is the home of great ideas and great things. America is the place where the car was born! America is the place where the computer was born! America is the place where Brad Paisley was born, for cryin' out loud! And if you believe my friend Carol, America is the place where Jesus was born! Is Carol here? Hi, Carol!

So how do we get this country on track again? Well, here's a start. As my first act in office, I have directed the Snuggie company to make a new Snuggie emblazoned with the American flag. Adding American jobs to make those new Snuggies and restoring American pride in the process! (pause for cheer—"American pride" is the ONLY kind of pride!) *And, yes, America, in my administration, every purchase of a Snuggie*

still *comes with the free reading light!* (pause for cheer—
people love free stuff)

*That's just the first step in what will be an immediate
restoration of American greatness after 4 years of leadership by
an Indonesian man who also happened to be black* (pause for
boos—people do not like minorities). *In my first hundred
days, which start pretty soon here, I will deliver on the three
promises I made to you before you sent me to Washington
through that magical process of electoral democracy imagined by
our forefathers, who were true patriots and also ensured our right
to keep and bear arms.* (pause for big cheer—people love
guns ;))

*Number 1, I will sign an executive order enacting my "Eye
for an Eye" policy on abortion: you abort an unborn child, we
abort you. Plain and simple.* (pause for big cheer—people
love catchy antiabortion slogans that can be put on
bumper stickers)

*Number 2, New York's Manhattan Island will be converted
into a penal colony, inhabited by America's worst of the worst:
Hollywood smut merchants, suspicious-looking cab drivers, and
high school biology teachers.* (pause for cheer—people don't
like New York City, home of liberals, gays, Muslims,
and Jewish people . . . and probably liberal, gay Muslim
Jews)

*Third, but certainly not least, I will construct a dome over
the United States of America to prevent those who would wish
harm on us from delivering on their terrorist promises.* (pause for

huge cheer—sports fans love domes!) *Creating jobs in the construction sector and defending America—that's what we call back in Alaska a "two-fer"!* (cheers) *True, there will no longer be sunlight in our great nation, but I ask you, what's more important: getting a nice suntan or protecting our freedoms?* (pause for cheer—the word "freedoms" really sets people off)

I'll spare you the other details on the economy and health care and all that jazz because an inauguration is not the time to discuss boring stuff. It's the time to celebrate the part of America that is not inhabited by the elites of Washington, New York, Los Angeles, and especially San Francisco, if you know what I mean. (pause for cheer—people do NOT like gays) *I hear Sgt. Slaughter gettin' ready back there so I'll wrap things up here by saying something I've been waiting 4 years to say: Hey, Katie Couric, you wanted to know what I read? Well, I'm president now, so look real close here, see if you can read this, biaaaaaatch!* (thrust middle finger in the air to wild cheers) *The Mama Grizzly is President!*

Thank you, Tampa! May God bless you and God bless the states of America that are worthy of his blessing! Todd and I are goin' to Dave and Buster's to play air hockey tonight if you want to join us! Jalapeño poppers are on us, America!

2

I'm Tiger Woods . . . and I'm an Addict

★

"Good evening, everyone. I'm Dr. Sabrina Vanden Fanny. I want to welcome you to the Wilton Norman Chamberlain Sexual Addiction Institute, Southern California's top treatment center for celebrity sex addiction, which, I would like to remind everyone, is an actual medical condition. I went to graduate school and everything.

"It's nice to see so many familiar faces in our circle tonight, although, I must say, it doesn't say much for our success in treating your very serious disease." The assembled celebrity sex addicts, seated in a circle of metal folding chairs, nod to greet the familiar Dr. Vanden Fanny.

"Remember, my friends, no matter what the public says, you are not garden-variety scumbags. You're victims of a terrible affliction that causes you to want to have sex with every carbon-based being that crosses your path."

Dr. Vanden Fanny, the middle-aged director of the Chamberlain Institute and a pioneer in sex addiction academic study, turns and gestures toward framed portraits on the wall behind her of presidents John F. Kennedy and William J. Clinton.

"Let's begin tonight's meeting, as we do every meeting, with a reminder of the greatness we all can achieve in spite of our crippling sex addiction. It doesn't have to be a death sentence, my friends. These two great American presidents stand as shining examples of the courage of our community."

Despite growing criticism from the press and the medical community that she and a group of fellow acupuncturists invented the field of "sex addiction research" as a means to exploit celebrities looking for a way out of public sex scandals, Dr. Vanden Fanny takes her work quite seriously.

"As you all know, we work every day here at the institute to bring an end to the addiction that struck Wilt Chamberlain and caused him to have sex with 20,000 women over the course of a tortured life. Wilt was derided as a lothario. He was mocked as an out-of-control Casanova. Some even called this gentle giant a 7-foot-tall sex beast. Today we know he was none of those things. He was a victim of sex addiction, plain and simple. And so we take Wilt's lifetime of torment and use it as our strength and motivation to find a cure in his name."

The group applauds. Dr. Vanden Fanny talks over the clapping, raising her voice to be heard.

"So, just to be clear, sex addiction is real. And we have a

center here in Malibu where we study it." Satisfied for the moment that her point has been made, she continues.

"As you all know, we are here tonight to welcome a new member into our Chamberlain family. And I use the word 'family' intentionally here—mainly because I don't want you to have sex with each other, and perhaps the idea that you are somehow family relatives would deter you. It's a long shot, I know.

"Anyhow, our new friend was delivered to us by his IMG management team two days ago after a long period of focus group testing to determine how he should handle his very public problems. We're awfully proud of him for admitting he's got some things he needs to work on and for being man enough to ask for help here at Chamberlain.

"I don't want to embarrass him, but I'm proud to say as we sit here tonight, he has not nailed a single member of our staff since he began treatment. Friends, please say hello to the PGA's 10-time Player of the Year—no pun intended—Tiger Woods."

The assembled sex addicts give Woods a standing ovation. Woods, dressed in a red golf shirt and black pants, stands and tips his cap as if walking up the 18th fairway at Augusta National.

"Thanks so much, Dr. Vanden Fanny. And thank you all." Woods takes a deep breath and blows it out slowly.

"I just want to say something I should have said a long time ago: my name is Tiger Woods and I'm a sex addict."

The group claps loudly and stands for Woods again. Tiger breaks into a wide toothy smile. Dr. Vanden Fanny puts her arm around the golf great and rubs his back.

"How does it feel, Tiger? How does it feel?"

Tiger chokes back tears. "It feels like I just won the Masters, Dr. Vanden Fanny. That's how it feels."

As the group applauds again, Tiger leans in so only Dr. Vanden Fanny can hear him. "But can you get your hand off my back? It's kind of making me want to bend you over that sink."

Dr. Vanden Fanny slides her hand off his back. "Of course, Tiger. I'm sorry. That's my fault. Not your fault. You have a disease. It's my fault." She turns back to the group.

"Tiger, that is the most important step of the process. You've just admitted that you are an addict. A real addict. Like a drug addict, except you're addicted to sex. The condition was mentioned on *Access Hollywood* earlier this week. It's real."

Tiger collects himself and looks out to the group, as Dr. Vanden Fanny continues.

"Now the next step is to meet your new family. Let's go around the circle, gang, introduce ourselves to Tiger, and make him feel welcome. Let's start right here with you, Gene."

KISS guitar god Gene Simmons touches his legendary tongue to his forehead before he speaks. "Tiger, great to have you here, brother. You've got nothing to be ashamed of, my man. Sex addiction is perfectly natural. Don't take my word for it—read the Bible. 'Spread thy seed . . .' Old Testament shit. It's not like I pulled it out of my ass. Richard Gere over there is the only one in this group pulling weird stuff out of his ass."

Richard Gere lets out a loud laugh and throws a used cardboard paper towel roll at Simmons in mock protest. Simmons ducks the flying object and continues.

"Love ya, Richard, you sick fuck! I gotta tell you though, Tiger, it's a long road to recovery on this thing. Every time I think I'm cured, I catch myself taking the top off my sweet little red Lamborghini and screwing the gas tank. Mmmmmm . . ."

Simmons sticks out his tongue and mimes the action he's describing. Dr. Vanden Fanny stops him. "Okay, thanks, Gene. Let's keep moving. Charlie?"

Charlie Sheen stands up. "Tiger, good to see you again, man. You may not remember this, but you and I were pounding the same waitress out in Vegas for a while."

Woods looks confused and says nothing.

"Jamie something-or-other? Bellagio? Monster rack?"

Woods does not respond.

"Guess she didn't tell you. Oops. Anyway, hello everyone. I'm Charlie Sheen from America's #1 comedy *Two and a Half Men* and I'm still not convinced I'm a sex addict." The group cannot contain its laughter.

"No, seriously, guys! I think I might just be an asshole. Like, I'm pretty sure I could stop myself, but I just don't fucking want to. Can we make up a medical condition to explain that? I-Don't-Give-a-Shit-itis, maybe?"

Dr. Vanden Fanny jumps in again. "I assure you, Charlie, as I've said many times, there is nothing 'made up' about sex addiction. There are a number of Internet blogs dedicated to the subject."

Sheen gives the international "jerk off" signal. Dr. Vanden Fanny points to the next person. A bearded man in full military regalia jumps to his feet.

"El Tigre! I know, I know, you're surprised to see the great Fidel Castro here with a bunch of amateurs. Thirty-five thousand women and counting, *amigo*! What'd you bang—15, 20 broads? That's a three-day weekend for me!" Castro leans back and extends his arms wide with a big laugh. He enjoys his own material.

Woods is indeed surprised to see the Cuban leader at the meeting of celebrity sex addicts. Castro stops laughing and a stern look crosses his face.

"And by the way, Dr. Vanden Fanny, it pisses me right off when you make us salute the photograph of Jack-off Kennedy before every meeting. That guy is supposed to be some kind of big sex symbol? Call me when he gets near 35,000, sweetheart. He banged one movie star. So what? And by the way, J. Edgar Hoover told me he had firsthand proof that Marilyn Monroe was a dude anyway. Long story.

"Oh, and wait, there's something else. Wait, what is it again? Oh yeah: I whipped his ass at the Bay of Pigs! Salute that, Vanden Fanny!"

Dr. Vanden Fanny allows Castro to continue without arguing the point.

"But this isn't about me, Tiger. It's about you. It's great to have you here with the rest of these horndogs." Castro points across the circle.

"I mean, Duchovny over there's got the hormones of a 16-year-old. And if I catch Angela Lansbury sitting on the washer during spin cycle again, I'm gonna call in the Cuban army to make it stop! Jesucristo!" Lansbury smiles and shrugs at the devilish Castro. Dr. Vanden Fanny shakes her head.

"All right, relax, Vanden Fanny, I'm finished here. One more thing, Tiger: when we're done with this little song and dance today, I could use some help off the tee. I'm spraying the ball all over the place. I need a goddamned Weedwacker to get out of the rough. I spend about as much time on the fairway as you spend with your wife."

Tiger responds, stone-faced, "I'd be happy to show you a couple of things, Fidel."

Castro quips, "Great. No pressure, but I've got a prison full of coaches who couldn't fix the hitch in my backswing."

Dr. Vanden Fanny moves things along. "Okay, El Jefé. No speeches today. Let's move on. Ted?"

A man wearing a maroon zip-up jacket stands reluctantly. Beads of sweat cover his brow and lip. He forces a wide, harsh smile that belies the deep sadness of his life.

"Well, uh, hello, Tiger. I am the Reverend Ted Haggard. As you may know, for a long time, I enjoyed crystal meth and the company of male hookers. Notice the past tense there."

Tiger recognizes Haggard vaguely from the news and nods.

"Just want you to know that the Lord has already forgiven you for your sins. He is pleased that you are working to save your soul here at the Chamberlain Institute.

"Unfortunately, I'm still waitin' to hear back from the Big Man Upstairs on my little situation." Haggard forces a short, hard laugh. No one else even smiles. It's all too sad.

"Turns out He's not quite as lenient with pastors who do meth with gay hookers at seedy motels in between sermons as I'd hoped He'd be." Haggard laughs for a few short moments before collapsing into his metal chair and sobbing uncontrollably.

Michael Douglas hugs Haggard, pulling the disgraced reverend's head into his chest. "Shhhhh! Shhhhhh! There you are, Ted. There you are, big guy. I'm sure there's a god somewhere who still loves you." Douglas winks at Dr. Vanden Fanny and gestures with his head to skip his turn while he comforts Haggard, who is slobbering all over Douglas's $15,000 Brioni suit.

Dr. Vanden Fanny tries to rouse the next member of the group.

"Paris?"

She gets no response.

"Paris?"

Still nothing. Dr. Vanden Fanny tries one last time.

"Paris?"

Hotel heiress Paris Hilton finally looks up from her iPhone. "What?"

"Paris, would you like to say hello to Tiger Woods?"

"I can't. I'm watching my sex tape again. It's so f'in hot."

As though prompted by a starter's pistol, R. Kelly and Ruth Bader Ginsburg bound out of their chairs and dart across the room to get a view of what Hilton is watching.

The exasperated Dr. Vanden Fanny presses a button, sounding a loud alarm. Within seconds, two uniformed orderlies rush into the room with Tasers. Kelly and Ginsburg are subdued and removed from the meeting.

Dr. Vanden Fanny shakes her head. "This is why we do *not* allow electronic devices in our meetings, folks." She turns and points to a large sign confirming the policy, posted clearly next to a portrait of Eleanor Roosevelt.

"I'm so sorry about that, Tiger. Let's continue with our introductions."

A bearded man with glasses rises to his feet.

"Hey ya, Tiger. Salman Rushdie. Yep, the guy everyone in the world is either trying to kill or hump. There's really no in-between there."

Tiger gives Rushdie a polite wave from across the room.

"Truth be told, I wasn't a sex addict until the whole fatwa thing. Honestly, I couldn't pay my Guatemalan housekeeper to go on a date with me until the Ayatollah told every Muslim nutjob in the world to kill me over a stupid book. I guess any publicity is good publicity, right?"

Tiger shakes his head. "No, actually."

Rushdie blows right past it. "Every time one of these guys tries to kill me, another supermodel shows up in my bed. It's unbelievable, man! I should have written that book when I was 17—maybe someone would have gone to the prom with me!" Rushdie laughs at his own line.

"All kidding aside, Tiger, it's great to have you here. Sex addiction is no joke—unless you're Louie Anderson over there," Rushdie points at comedian and former *Family Feud* host Louie Anderson.

"Louie's been begging for somebody to put a fatwa on him. He hasn't had sex with anything that doesn't require batteries in about 15 years. Am I right, Louie?" Anderson lets out a big laugh and throws a D battery at Rushdie.

Dr. Vanden Fanny has seen just about enough.

"It's clear everyone is a little loopy today, so why don't we wrap this up and we'll get Tiger back to his sensory-deprivation tank for the night."

She waits for the celebrity patients to settle. When there is quiet she continues.

"Tiger, look around this room. These are your brothers and sisters in the fight against a disease that 21 percent of readers in a *USA Today* online poll called 'probably legit.' This is your family. We're small, but we're awfully strong. I find myself learning from these brave fighters each and every day. The men and women of the Chamberlain Institute are bound together by an addiction to wild, inventive, ass-slapping sex, but they refuse to be defined by their condition."

As Tiger listens, he scans the collection of sex-addicted celebrities, smiling, nodding, and daydreaming about the defining time he had wild, inventive, ass-slapping sex in a waitress's mini-van in the parking lot of an Orlando-area Shoney's.

While the likes of Sarah Palin, Tiger Woods, and Lindsay Lohan hog the headlines, brave, everyday Americans with names you would not recognize toil in the shadows, making their small, daily contributions to the American Freak Show. You'll find some of their inspirational true stories sprinkled throughout this book. Read them to your children. Tell the next generation tales of this glorious city upon a hill we call America. Tales like this one . . .

TRUE STORY . . .

DRAG QUEEN ROBS BURGER KING
Cross-dresser holds up New Orleans fast food joint

You have to admire a criminal who, in preparing to commit his crime, stops to consider the poetic newspaper headline that will announce it the next day. A criminal like the drag queen who robbed a Burger King in New Orleans.

The six-foot one-inch man wearing a wig, a dress, and matching jewelry pulled up in the drive-thru lane late one night, got out of his pickup truck, and climbed through the service window with a gun in his hand. The well-appointed armed robber cleaned out the registers—leaving behind a bounty of delicious BK Triple Stackers in his haste—and made his escape back out the drive-thru window.

So how do we know this was a case of honest-to-goodness cross-dressing and not just an elaborate criminal disguise? Why, just ask New Orleans crime and safety specialist Howard Robertson: "Most of the time when somebody puts on a wig they're just trying to hide their identity by putting on something like a Halloween mask, but he's pretty," Robertson said in an actual quote.

One assumes that many of the cross-dressing armed robber's fellow inmates find him just as pretty as crime and safety specialist Howard Robertson does.

3

"They Think He's Jesus": Hillary's Private Campaign E-mails

★

I'd love to tell you that the following e-mails were obtained through the Freedom of Information Act or something official-sounding like that. It turns out, however, that the public does not have the freedom of information shared privately between a husband and wife. Especially this husband and wife.

So the truth is that my friend Heath, who's great with computers (worked on the Best Buy Geek Squad for a while), hacked into the Hotmail server and monitored Hillary and Bill Clinton's private e-mail exchanges for several months before he was caught and sent to a secret prison in Romania. What follows are the handful of e-mails Heath copied and sent to me before he was thrown into a potato sack and heaved into the back of a van while leaving a TCBY in Fresno on the afternoon of October 21, 2008. No one has heard from him since.

If you can ignore the fact that the messages were obtained illegally, you'll find they provide fascinating insight into the Clintons' state of mind and behind-the-scenes movements during key moments of the 2008 presidential campaign. These documents are an important (and, again, entirely illegal) addition to the historical record. I should tell you upfront that just by reading the e-mails, you are complicit in the crime and could face criminal prosecution and extraordinary rendition. Enjoy!

Reader's Guide

Presidential candidate Hillary Clinton = IShouldBePresident@hotmail.com

President Bill Clinton = BubbaHeartsTail69@hotmail.com

The following e-mails were written between January 1 and January 4, 2008, during the Iowa caucuses.

To: BubbaHeartsTail69@hotmail.com
From: IShouldBePresident@hotmail.com
Re: IOWA
January 1, 2008

Hi Bill . . . Happy New Year! What'd you get into last night? I took it easy, watched the ball drop with the staff. BTW, that Ryan Seacrest is adorable and has broad appeal (can you say Veep short list?). We're just restin' up now to whip BO and pretty boy Edwards' asses in a couple days.

Cannot WAIT to get out of Iowa. If I wanted to spend all my time around a bunch of dumb hicks I would have stayed in Arkansas with you and the rest of the hillbillies. Can we just cut the bullshit now and go straight to the inauguration, please?! Don't want to get too far ahead of myself yet (because those Republican challengers are so daunting—McCain? Huckabee? Ooooooooooh, scaryyyy!), but for music at the Inaugural Ball I'm going back and forth between Carly Simon (too mellow?) and Tina Turner (too Obamaish?). Thoughts? And, no, Barbra Streisand is not invited.

Don't forget: I have that decorator meeting us at the WH on Wednesday to talk fabrics for the Oval Office. (Still so crazy to think—FIRST WOMAN PRESIDENT! AHHHHH!!!!) Anyway, definitely want some female touches. We're taking down Bush's Roger Staubach posters. And we need to get the BBQ stains steamed out of the carpets. See ya there—key's still under the planter at North Portico.

To: IShouldBePresident@hotmail.com
From: BubbaHeartsTail69@hotmail.com
Re: Re: IOWA
January 1, 2008

Hey, HRC. Not much last night for New Year's. You know, just guy stuff. I was gonna watch *Varsity Blues* (again!) and go to bed early, but then a few of the fellas decided we oughta road trip to Vegas. They're very persuasive! Long story short, I'm watching the Capital One Bowl at the Caesar's Sports Book with some terrific folks I met last night. Ever drink a yard glass full of strawberry daiquiri? I hadn't until a minute ago!

Don't sweat Iowa. Take a look at the faces in those crowds: they are NOT voting for Barack Obama. He reminds those people of O.J. It's Honky Central out there. This one's in the bag, Hillary! (And so am I! ☺)

To: BubbaHeartsTail69@hotmail.com
From: IShouldBePresident@hotmail.com
Re: Re: IOWA
January 3, 2008

Just lost Iowa. Came in third. For reals. They don't think he's O.J. They think he's Jesus.

To: IShouldBePresident@hotmail.com
From: BubbaHeartsTail69@hotmail.com
Re: Re: IOWA
January 4, 2008

What?! Damn! Sorry, I missed the vote last night. We were driving up to Tahoe. No phones/TV. You know how it is. Don't worry, I got whipped in Iowa and look at me now: beloved two-term president barnstorming across Nevada with Bret Michaels in an RV full of A-list porn stars! Hang in there.

Will call when I can, but, again, terrible phone reception, etc. Trying to lay the groundwork for that Nevada primary, but if cocktail waitresses are any indication, the service employees are going for Barry O. They love that dude! Really starting to piss me off, actually. Don't worry, I'm workin' on 'em (if you know what I mean ;)). They'll come around to Big Poppa.

p.s.—I won $25K and a Corvette in a celebrity poker tournament in Reno! Kind of a split decision for the Clintons last night, I guess. . . .

The following e-mails were written between January 7 and January 9, 2008, during the New Hampshire primary.

To: BubbaHeartsTail69@hotmail.com
From: IShouldBePresident@hotmail.com
Re: NEW HAMPSHIRE
January 7, 2008

If I lose in NH, I'm done. Everyone thinks BO is going to win. Need something dramatic. Trying to remind everyone that he's a black guy who loves blow. What else?

To: IShouldBePresident@hotmail.com
From: BubbaHeartsTail69@hotmail.com
Re: Re: NEW HAMPSHIRE
January 7, 2008

You know that bullshit where I bite my bottom lip and squint my eyes to show I care? Works every time, man. Try it. Don't slobber all over yourself—people will think you're a crazy bitch who shouldn't be anywhere near the red button. Just tear up a little bit. Feel their pain. Trust me.

Trying to get back to NH for tomorrow. All the flights from Aspen are snowed in. Met some really cool people who are insisting I stay for their key party tomorrow night. Kinda said I would. Will let you know if I can get out of it.

In the meantime, I'm spreadin' the word through our back channels that BO is a giant Indonesian cokehead. Moral high ground's a little tough for me, but doing my best. Off to the slopes! Talk soon.

To: BubbaHeartsTail69@hotmail.com
From: IShouldBePresident@hotmail.com
Re: Re: NEW HAMPSHIRE
January 7, 2008

Going to a coffee shop in Portsmouth now. Will try the tears there. Have been going with the whole tough woman thing, but at this point, fuck it. I hope this works better than your last idea about bringing up Obama's "I Want to Become President" kindergarten essay. That sucked balls.

Oh, and not that you care, but I am NOT cool with you going to a key party in Aspen.

To: IShouldBePresident@hotmail.com
From: BubbaHeartsTail69@hotmail.com
Re: Re: NEW HAMPSHIRE
January 8, 2008

Jack Nicholson and Woody Harrelson having an NH primary viewing party at Jack's place. Probably just gonna crash there tonight. Cool? Thanks. You're the best. Good luck!

To: BubbaHeartsTail69@hotmail.com
From: IShouldBePresident@hotmail.com
Re: Re: NEW HAMPSHIRE
January 9, 2008

I WON! I got choked up and I won, goddamn it! I'm back, baby! How ya like me now, Obama!! DO NOT FUCK WITH ME!!!!!!

BTW, where are you? Haven't heard from you since yesterday. Got a phone message at 3:30 a.m. that I thought was going to be you congratulating me, but was 4 minutes of you and Nicholson talking to some University of Colorado cheerleaders about your administration's achievements in women's rights. You "fought to uphold a woman's right to show her love for another woman in public"? Pathetic. Yeah, I heard that. You must have sat on your BlackBerry and called me. Not good, dude.

To: IShouldBePresident@hotmail.com
From: BubbaHeartsTail69@hotmail.com
Re: Re: NEW HAMPSHIRE
January 9, 2008

CONGRATS!!! Meant to call you last night, but got caught up talking policy with the gang from the Aspen Institute. Mostly fiscal responsibility, NATO expansion, etc. Boring stuff. That's who those people on my message were. Totally not Colorado cheerleaders. Just cheerleaders for America's future! Right?

OK, I'm gonna try to catch a flight out to meet you. Let's go win this nomination! BTW, Cheryl Tiegs is a big fan of yours!

To: IShouldBePresident@hotmail.com
From: BubbaHeartsTail69@hotmail.com
Re: Re: NEW HAMPSHIRE
January 9, 2008

Hey Melissa. I have an entirely new appreciation for cheerleading. WOW!

So, I've gotta go do some BS campaign stuff with Hillary. I know, total bummer. She has literally NO chance of winning, but gotta keep up appearances. Back in town soon. Will call. Go Buffs!

To: BubbaHeartsTail69@hotmail.com
From: IShouldBePresident@hotmail.com
Re: Re: NEW HAMPSHIRE
January 9, 2008

WHAT IS THIS? WHO IS MELISSA?!

To: IShouldBePresident@hotmail.com
From: BubbaHeartsTail69@hotmail.com
Re: Re: NEW HAMPSHIRE
January 9, 2008

Oops! Totally sent that to the wrong person. Just following up with one of the senior fellows at Aspen Institute. My bad! See you soon, Hills.

The following e-mails were written on February 5, 2008, the primary day known as Super Tuesday.

To: BubbaHeartsTail69@hotmail.com
From: IShouldBePresident@hotmail.com
Re: SUPER TUESDAY!
February 5, 2008

Big wins tonight. We're still alive! I won the real states (CA and NY) and BO won a bunch more that don't have running water or people with teeth. Whatever.

I know all that stuff you said in South Carolina was bad and everything, but I think you made the country finally wake up and realize BO is a black guy! Time to get real, America. This isn't *American Idol,* you illiterate dipshits! IT'S THE GODDAMNED PRESIDENCY!!!

BTW, we're trying to come up with a list of scary black guys to compare Obama to. So far we have: Mike Tyson, 50 Cent, Louis Farrakhan, Suge Knight, and that huge guy from *Green Mile.* More?

To: IShouldBePresident@hotmail.com
From: BubbaHeartsTail69@hotmail.com
Re: Re: SUPER TUESDAY!
February 5, 2008

Glad all my work out here in American Samoa paid off! Been beatin' the bushes for two weeks. We earned this one!

Crazy story: after a long night of drinking coconut rum at a Get Out the Vote rally in Pago Pago, I found myself in a wild threesome that lasted for what seemed like days. Before you get ticked off, hear me out. As the political gods would have it: my new friends turned out to be . . . drum roll please . . . American Samoa's TWO DELEGATES! What are the odds?! Gal named Shannon and a neat local fella by the name of Marcel. Let's just say they were on the fence going in and "solidly Clinton" afterward. Classic retail politics, right? This really was a SUPER Tuesday! Ha!

Oh, and on the black guy thing, Obama reminds me of Snoop Dogg: tall, skinny, wily, and likes drugs. Go with it.

The following e-mail was written in the early morning hours of June 1, 2008, the day of the Puerto Rico primary.

To: BubbaHeartsTail69@hotmail.com
From: IShouldBePresident@hotmail.com
Re: PUERTO RICO
June 1, 2008

Yes, Bill, I know it's 2:30 a.m., and, yes, I am drunk-mailing from San Juan right now. This race is so over. Soooooooo over. I only came down here to sit in the sun and blow the rest of the campaign money on a giant Ricky Martin concert. That guy is such a flamer. It's not even clear to me that Puerto Ricans are allowed to vote in our elections. Are they? I always forget.

So, whoopee, Hillary Clinton has 18 million votes! Great! She put cracks in the glass ceiling! Yayyyyy! Funny, I don't see any of those 18 million people right now. The only two people in this room are me and Jose Cuervo. Oh, and I think that's Ed Rendell passed out in the bathtub. It's been a weird night.

I wonder if this is what it was like for Elvis at the end. All the fame and money in the world meant nothing as he sat alone on the can with a bottle of pills. It all means NOTHING! Or maybe this is what Hitler felt like alone in that bunker before he capped himself.

I can't believe J.Lo didn't endorse me. Ricky Martin's endorsement was nice, but it would have been even nicer . . . if I were running for president in 1999!!! Is Shakira Puerto Rican? Who knows.

OK, I'm rambling. Bottom line: campaign is over. The dream is dead. All that for nothing. And by "all that," I mean "my entire life." You win, Bill, OK? YOU WIN AGAIN! You're the president everybody loves. You can do no wrong. And I'm just the mean lady who blew it. I'm the inevitable candidate who lost to a BLACK GUY! I lost to a black guy from Indonesia who loves cocaine, for Christ's sake! Do you know what this means? There's gonna be a black president and it's my fault. I'm so voting for McCain. He'd have to pick, like, Miss Alaska as his running mate to lose my vote at this point. Ha!

Now if you'll excuse us, my 18 million votes and I are going down to the hotel bar for another round of piña coladas and video poker.

4

Lindsay Lohan: Twitter from a Santa Monica Jail

★

After her most recent arrest on charges of DUI and possession of a controlled substance, actress Lindsay Lohan authored a series of Tweets from her temporary holding cell at the jail in Santa Monica, California. In the spirit of a similar manifesto written by Dr. Martin Luther King Jr. during his confinement in Birmingham nearly half a century earlier, Lohan's Tweets serve as a mission statement, a call to action, and a loud cry for justice not just here at home, but around the world.

lindsaylohan *SUX! Just got arrested for Dooey. Why peeps constantly want to tear LL down?! Not cool. Someone bail me out! Usual spot. ONE LUV, y'all . . .*

lindsaylohan *Obv. not psyched to be in this cell, but seriously you guyz, policemen are the real heroes. Remember 9/11. Officer here a huge Freaky Friday fan. LOL.*

lindsaylohan *BTW, wasn't kidding about bailing me out. Supposed to be at after-party for Cash Warren's cologne launch in like 15 mins. Hurry, plz.*

lindsaylohan *OMG! Courtney Love is 2 cells down. So love her personal style. We're communicating by banging our chow pans on the floor. Total Shawshank right now!*

lindsaylohan *U can't even understand unless you've been here the racial disparity in our jails. So messed up. ReTweet to everyone you know & let's change the world.*

lindsaylohan *Ewwww! Courtney just tried to sell me to some super-sketchy chick for a pack of cigarettes. Not cool. Such a reminder: be good to each other, guyz . . .*

lindsaylohan *Hate myself for saying this, but DYING to give this one guard a LiLo makeover! Can tell she's HOTTT underneath her off-the-rack police costume . . .*

lindsaylohan *I honestly can't remember why I'm in jail. Kinda f'd up. Does anyone know? Check TMZ. It's hotter than Criss Angel's ballz in here! Not that I'd no ;)*

lindsayfan54 @lindsaylohan *We LUV U Lindz!!!! Cops say U wr arrested fr driving 120 mph wrng way down PCH. Also bag of coke in ur glove comprtmnt. Stay strng, grl!*

lindsaylohan *Thx, LindsayFan54! Celebrity is a dbl-edge sord. Media/ cops out to get LL again. Would normal person be in jail for speeding tickt? Think about it, guyz.*

lindsaylohan *So much time to reflect in here. Want to live/love better. Plus so much suffering in world. So sad. Also, thinking about going back to brunette? Yay or nay?!*

lindsaylohan *Been here 30 mins & starting to feel hopelessness other celebs—Mandela, Gandi, O.J.—must have felt. They take evrything from you (excpt BBerry ☺)*

lindsaylohan *Is it possible Im getting more f'd up as i sit here? Took weird green pills right before cops pulled me. So proud of this country for electing black man president.*

lindsaylohan *Guyz, it's up to our generation to stop global warming. Do your part, OK? Had so much fun working on Parent Trap. RIP, Natasha Richardson (aka "MOM").*

lindsaylohan *Seriously, guyz. Anyone coming to get me? TP in here is mad harsh. So much of the 3rd world lives in terrible poverty while we drnk champagne. THINK.*

lindsaylohan *My designer friend Joaquin Calebra has sick new line of bags. Check out: http://tinyurl.com/3rsfg. Small % of proceeds to orphanage in N. Korea. Heartbrking.*

lindsaylohan *Anyone remember how Tango & Cash escaped from prison? Need 2 get the f out uv here. Hair/makup not allwd in cell. Total deprivation. Cherish what u have, guyz.*

lindsaylohan *Check out this TwitPic of me in here. Not prtty, but the wrld has to no what prison does to a person. If my example frees 1 person frm death row its worth it.*

lindsaylohan *How 2 keep faith/hope/sanity in here? Closing eyes & remembring St. Barts with Kate Moss on Jerry Bruckheimer's yacht ovr MLK weekend this yr. Tru happiness.*

lindsaylohan *Every minute I rot in here, a thousand more acres of rain forest r cleared by big business & Halliburton & LL can't do anything about it. No blood 4 oil, Cheney!*

lindsaylohan *!!!! Some random stalker-dude just bailed me out!!! Looks drty & crcked out, borderline homeless, but in hott young Keith Richards way. YUM!*

lindsaylohan *Learned so much about myself in jail. Definitely changes U & ur priorities. Want to work w/ poor/fat people . . . but first Cash's after-party! PEACE & LOVE, guyz!*

TRUE STORY . . .

"IT'S MY LAWNMOWER. I CAN SHOOT IT IF I WANT TO"
Drunk man arrested for shooting lawnmower

57-year-old Keith Walendowski was minding his own business one spring morning, drinking beer, basking in the warm sun, and shooting his lawnmower with a sawed-off shotgun, when officers from the Milwaukee Police Department arrived to question him. Turns out a nosy neighbor had called to report shots fired from the direction of Walendowski's backyard.

According to the criminal complaint, Walendowski explained the noise very simply. "I'll tell you the truth," he told police. "I got pissed because my lawnmower wouldn't start, so I got my shotgun and shot it. It's my lawnmower and my yard, so I can shoot it if I want." Damn right.

Despite his seemingly flawless constitutional defense, Walendowski was charged with a felony count of possessing a short-barreled shotgun and a misdemeanor count of disorderly conduct while armed.

Keith Walendowski's is a cautionary tale. A country where a man cannot get liquored up at 9:30 in the morning and shoot a lawnmower in his own backyard has come unmoored from its founding principles of individual freedom and inebriation. First they came for the sawed-off shotguns, America.

5

Obama vs. Cheney: Late Night in the White House Kitchen

★

President Barack Obama is jolted awake by the sound of a crash. He sits up in bed and waits in still silence to hear it again, but nothing. The president turns to see the first lady sleeping, unfazed by the noise. Maybe it was just the sound of the overnight staff moving about downstairs, he thought. Or perhaps it was nothing more than the drafty old White House whistling its two-hundred-year-old song. Whatever it was, Obama resents having been woken from a wonderful dream in which he was riding a bicycle built for two along Lake Michigan with his beloved friend and unrepentant terrorist Bill Ayres.

The clock on the nightstand in the president's White House bedroom reads 3:37 a.m. He puts his head back on the pillow.

Then, before he can slip back into unconsciousness, an even louder crash—the unmistakable sound of a plate smashing on a hard floor. Obama springs up from bed. This is no dream. The first lady rolls over, looking up at her husband.

"Did you hear that?" he asks.

"Did you lock the back door before you went to bed?" she whispers.

"Damn it!" Obama smacks himself on the forehead.

Exasperated by the president's recent negligence of basic household responsibilities, the first lady shoots back, "Well, get down there and see what it is." She rolls back over on her pillow. "And sort the recycling while you're down there—like I asked you yesterday."

The president peels back the covers and climbs out of bed. He is wearing the "I ♥ Big Government" pajamas given to him as a birthday gift by his old Republican colleague in the Senate Dick Lugar. (Lugar, as you may know, is Capitol Hill's king of gag gifts. In the midst of the Lewinsky scandal, he sent Bill Clinton a box of exploding cigars with a humorous note reading, "This one really blew up in your face, didn't it?! Yours, Big Dick.")

Obama grabs a 7-iron out of the golf bag left in a closet by Dwight Eisenhower and tiptoes his way out of the room to confront whomever—or whatever—is making the noise. As the president slides down the grand stairwell with his back against the wall, he sees a faint light reaching into the hallway from under the kitchen door. A couple of delicate, bare footsteps closer and he hears low murmuring—a man's voice. The president clutches the club tighter and suddenly reconsiders his position on gun control. A loaded semiautomatic handgun would be great right now, he thinks.

With the loud clanking of silverware now just on the other side of the kitchen door, the president braces himself, with both hands on the club, to face the intruder who has violated the sanctity of the American People's home. He closes his eyes and counts quietly, "1 . . . 2 . . . 3!"

"Hey!" the president shouts as he springs into the kitchen ready to fight.

The silhouette of an older, heavyset man standing at the kitchen's island is lit from behind only by the small light of the microwave. The man throws up his hands, dropping a butter knife from one and a sandwich from the other.

"Whoa! Whoa! Easy there, Tiger Woods! It's me!"

The president, with the golf club still poised, squints to see the man, but the room is too dark. He reaches behind him and turns on the overhead light. Standing there in the middle of the White House kitchen, wearing only a T-shirt and extraordinarily small white Jockey underwear, is Dick Cheney.

"What the f★★k?" the stunned president mutters under his breath.

Cheney breaks into a crooked smile. "Can I put my hands down here, officer? You already ruined my sandwich, and I don't mind telling you, you ruined this pair of underwear, too."

Obama lowers the club. "What the hell are you doing here, Vice President Cheney? It's three-thirty in the morning. And you're wearing your underwear. Jesus Christ, you scared the crap out of us."

Cheney lowers his arms. "First things first: call me Dick. Everybody else in your socialist party does," the former vice president quips with a laugh.

The look on Obama's face suggests that Cheney's attempted icebreaker has failed to break the considerably thick ice.

"Aw, phooey, did I wake you up when I dropped that plate? I apologize. I'm just having a little late-night snack here in my kitchen. That's my bad on the noise. Hey, how great is this T-shirt?"

Cheney pulls down his shirt to reveal the words I'M WITH STUPID and a photograph of President George W. Bush.

"Lugar gave it to me," he says with a chuckle.

Obama does not laugh. "Why are you in the White House, Dick? This is not your kitchen."

Cheney has turned back to his sandwich, spreading mayonnaise on a slice of bread. "I live here, Barack-Attack! We don't like to make a big fuss about it on account of the press would go batshit, but, yeah, got a little underground setup downstairs here. You wanna go check it out? I've got Xbox on the big screen and everything. Only downside is that we have to ride the dumbwaiter to get down there."

Obama puts the club down on the island and walks toward Cheney. "You live in the White House?! This is an outrage!"

Cheney takes a bite of the sandwich, stuffing a loose piece of lettuce into the side of his mouth. "Oh, spare me, Obama! I've been running the United States government since I got

Scalia to give Slappy the Clown that 2000 election. Would you believe that whole crazy thing was decided over a late-night game of pinochle at Newt's place? You tell anybody that, I'll have you sent to a black site in Siberia. No shit. I will do that."

Obama shakes his head as Cheney continues.

"Don't look so shocked, my man. Have you happened to notice that your foreign policy looks exactly like Slappy's? Well, you can thank your old Uncle Dick for that. Yes, sir. Still calling the shots down there."

Obama is stunned. "Good God!"

Cheney turns and opens the refrigerator, takes a swig of milk directly from the gallon jug. "And, look, I'm sorry for being an asshole to you all the time." Cheney wipes away the milk around his mouth. "I have to do that every now and again to throw everyone off the scent. I start praising you and people wonder what the hell's going on between us. That's why all the 'dithering' and 'He's making us less safe' ranting and raving. Are you mad at me?"

Obama does appear to be mad now.

"'Mad' is not the word, Dick. You are running my presidency from a room underneath the White House—"

Cheney jumps in, "Not just yours, Obama-Rama. Remember, I ran Slappy's, too. He started sobbing like a little girl on 9/11 and I took the wheel from there. Every time he got his courage up and asked to be included in a big decision, we'd tell him, 'The grown-ups are talking,' and send him to Crawford to clear brush for a couple of weeks. I know how that sounds, but trust me, it was better for everybody."

Obama speaks slowly and in a stern tone: "Mr. Cheney, I think you should finish that sandwich, go downstairs, pack up your things, and be on your way before I call the Secret Service."

Cheney lets out a hearty laugh. "The Secret Service?! Those guys love me. Besides, you're not gonna tell anyone. You want the world to know you're not really the president? Sure, let's go ahead and give *The Washington Post* the scoop right now. Who should I call, Woodward or Bernstein? Come on, Bam-Bam, get real!

"Plus, I ain't going anywhere until my bacon and cheddar Hot Pocket's done in the microwave. That is non-negotiable."

Obama concedes the condition. "Very well. You can wait until your Hot Pocket is ready." The president folds his arms and stares at Cheney as the Hot Pocket rotates in the soft light of the microwave over his shoulder. Cheney smacks his gut, looks up at the ceiling, and exhales. "Sooooo, this is awkward. How 'bout those Bears! Butkus is having another good year, huh?" Obama remains expressionless.

Cheney's face lights up with a thought. "Hey, do you know about *The Book*?"

Obama shakes his head. "What book?"

Cheney throws up his hands. "You seriously don't know about *The Book*? Oh, you're in for a treat. Have you ever seen the movie *American Pie* with that babe Tara Reid?"

Obama shakes his head again. "I have not."

Cheney breaks into a wide smile. "Oh, it's a really terrific coming-of-age story. You oughta rent the tape. So there's this part in there where the high school seniors pass down a book full of secrets and advice every year to the next class. Well, the outgoing class here at the White House does the same thing. It's all in *The Book*. Just like in *American Pie*."

Obama is mildly intrigued. "Is Tara Reid the one who's had the ongoing struggle with her personal body image?"

Cheney points at Obama. "That's her!"

Obama nods. "Oh yeah, she's very good."

Cheney ignores the microwave, whose beeping indicates the Hot Pocket is ready. "I think you're ready to see *The Book*, Tommy Barama. Technically, you are a president, I guess. Even if you *were* born in some terrorist hotbed."

He walks toward a shelf full of cookbooks and pulls away two of them. He reaches into the gap left by the books and comes out with a beautiful, red leather–bound volume embroidered in gold. Cheney wipes away a thin layer of dust on the book's cover to reveal the title *The Book*.

"Here it is, BO: *The Book*! Wisdom from all the presidents who have lived in this house. Unfortunately we only have the volume from the last one hundred years or so because that cocksucker Grover Cleveland took the first one home with him when he left office. You become the only guy to serve two nonconsecutive terms and suddenly you think your shit doesn't stink. The whole 'I'm the twenty-second *and* twenty-fourth president' thing went straight to his head."

Cheney hands the book to Obama and walks back to the microwave to retrieve his snack. "If it's just the same to you, I'm gonna take my snack back downstairs and catch the lottery drawing. I played the Pick Six tonight with the nuclear codes. Feelin' lucky! Hey, enjoy the book. There are some gems in there."

With that, the former vice president, wearing his T-shirt and snug tighty-whities, takes his Hot Pocket and stuffs himself into the dumbwaiter, descending slowly into the bowels of the White House from which he controls the United States government.

President Obama, standing in his pajamas in the darkness of the kitchen at four o'clock in the morning, opens *The Book* and, by the light of a microwave still warm from Dick Cheney's bacon and cheddar Hot Pocket, meets the ghosts of the White House past.

WILLIAM "BILL" McKINLEY

June 14, 1897

For the record, the last asshole, Grover Cleveland "Steamer," stole the first volume of "The Book." That's okay, Grover, I'm sure future presidents would have no interest in the wisdom of Washington, Jefferson, or Lincoln. Dick move, man. Dick move.

December 14, 1898

Get out the sunblock and fire up the margarita machine because I just took Puerto Rico, a bunch of the West Indies, Guam, and the Philippines from Spain! They call it the Spanish-American War, but trust me, it wasn't much of a war. More like four months of looking at island property in the Caribbean. See you in San Juan!

THEODORE ROOSEVELT

SEPTEMBER 15, 1901

Well, I guess McKinley isn't gonna get to chill in San Juan after all. He's chillin' in the morgue right now. Some crazy anarchist popped a cap in him. Fuckin' anarchists. Anyway, guess what this means? I'm president! I have no idea what I'm doing. Seriously. Don't tell anyone! ☺

APRIL 22, 1903

If you're reading this book it's too late for you, but this job kind of blows. I used to do tons of cool stuff—I was police chief in New York City, governor of New York, I led the Rough Riders up that hill—but this is booooooooring. I think I might go dig a canal for shits and giggles.

NOVEMBER 7, 1906

Okay, started the canal. It's gonna be kick-ass. Now they want me to get excited about the Meat Inspection Act. Meat Inspection?! I don't mean to big-time anybody, but do they know who I am? BTW, that would be a hilarious name for a porn film—The Meat Inspection Act. Ha! I'm so not running for reelection. I'm going to shoot elephants in Africa instead. Smell ya L8TR!!!!!

WILLIAM H. TAFT

JANUARY 1, 1913

It's been a heck of a ride here in the White House, but I just have to say, I did NOT get stuck in the goddamned bathtub! Seriously, you guys. That's an ugly smear spread by opponents who would rather focus on my weight than on the issues. Could I lose a few pounds? Sure. Could I stand to skip a few trips to the buffet? Of course. Does that mean I get stuck in bathtubs? Absolutely not. I'm gonna be SO pissed if the spurious bathtub story overshadows the legislative achievements of my historically great presidency. Do you think the Sixteenth Amendment passed itself?!

WOODROW WILSON

FEBRUARY 24, 1913

Dude, Taft totally got stuck in that bathtub. I hate to tell tales out of school, but I have it on good authority. It happened. They brought in the National Guard.

JUNE 28, 1919

Let's see, what did I do today? Oh yeah, I ended the Great War! Signed a treaty in the morning and by five o'clock I was four bottles of Lafite deep with Clemenceau celebrating world peace. All in a day's work. (I know it sounds like a cliché, but Paris really is beautiful this time of year if you get the chance to go.) Oh, and don't worry, you won't be hearing from those dumb Krauts anytime soon! Buried 'em at Versailles! There is absolutely no chance of a horrific backlash that will lead to the rise of a genocidal madman and haunt the world for centuries to come. You can thank me later.

AUGUST 18, 1920

To all the ladies in the house: let's not forget who got you the right to vote today. You're welcome, girls.

WARREN G. HARDING

JULY 19, 1923

My advice? Stay away from Teapot Domes! Jesus Christ, who knew anyone would give a shit? Totally misread that one. Also, I haven't been feeling well lately. If, God forbid, anything should ever happen to me, go easy on Coolidge. He doesn't say much, but he really is a sweet man.

**NOTE: President Harding died in office of a heart attack two weeks after writing this entry.

CALVIN COOLIDGE

AUGUST 4, 1923

Oh great, I'm president! I did not sign up for this shit! I'm not a people person at all. Ugh. So pissed right now . . .

AUGUST 27, 1928

We just signed the Kellogg-Briand Pact ending war everywhere forever. No more wars. Ever. Anywhere. Not bad, huh? Call me "Silent Cal" all you want, but I just ended fucking wars forever. Did I say that loud enough, bitch? There will never be another war ever again because of me. Everyone promised. I got it all in writing. Who's silent now?

HERBERT HOOVER

OCTOBER 29, 1929

OH SHIT!!!!!!!!!!!!!! Can't talk—I think the world economy just collapsed. This is not good.

FEBRUARY 21, 1930

Note to future presidents: you get blamed for shit you had nothing to do with. I hadn't even unpacked my cotton-pickin' Dopp kit yet when the stock market crashed and it's somehow all my fault? Everyone's like, "Do something, Hoover!" and I'm like, "Fucking call Coolidge, man! I've been here for five minutes, dude." So ol' Herbie Hoover's a big joke now while that cock Coolidge plays with himself on a beach somewhere. I'll tell ya, I must be a pretty damn effective president if I single-handedly orchestrated a global economic meltdown in the first 8 months of my presidency. That's some feat. This is such bullshit. I want out.

MAY 31, 1932

This sucks! People chase me down the street with pitchforks and torches like they do mythical ogres. Homeless people live in shantytowns named after me. I was hoping to save the name Hooverville for my presidential theme park back home. Guess I can forget that now. This is not going well at all. I'm running a half-assed reelection campaign before I turn this clusterfuck over to Roosevelt. It's all yours, Frank. Good luck!

FRANKLIN DELANO ROOSEVELT

MARCH 15, 1945

Sorry I haven't written sooner. Been a little busy, as you may have read in your history books. Just got back from Yalta and had a minute to write in "The Book." I guess as I look back, I really have only two small achievements to put down in writing: saving the world economy and freeing the planet of tyranny. You know, generally restoring our faith in humanity. Good luck living up to that legacy, guys.

Now, I respect the shit out of Abe Lincoln, as anyone who knows me will tell you, but honestly, you'd have to move me past him at this point on any list of Greatest American Presidents. We both healed the country, yes. But unless I missed something, I'm the only one of the two of us who healed the WORLD. Defeating both the Depression and that little fuck Hitler is a hell of a day's work, if you don't mind my saying. True, I gave myself a couple extra terms to get it all done, but I did it nevertheless. BTW, keep an eye on that

Stalin. We look good together in a Yalta class photo, but there's something about those Russkies I don't trust. I feel like he's hiding something behind that bushy porn 'stache.

Couple other things you should know: I had a pool installed at the White House to "help with my back." And by "help with my back" I mean "bang my secretary." Great spot to bring broads if you're into that kind of thing. Also, just for the historical record: my wife is not a dyke. I've heard the whispers. She's just a little homely. Explains the need for the swimming pool.

Well, off to Warm Springs soon with the secretary for a little extramarital sex and planning for the next 12 years of my presidency. Thinking about turning Japan into a horrific moonscape with these little doozies I've got a Jewish fella named Oppenheimer whippin' up for me. More on that when we get back.

p.s.—Not sure how I show up in photographs, but I am literally paralyzed. No one even knows that. So not only did I save the world, I did it without the ability to walk or stand. Pretty sure Stinkin' Lincoln didn't do that.

HARRY S. TRUMAN

May 8, 1945

Not saying it's all my doing, but is it a coincidence that I take over the presidency and four weeks later Hitler offs himself and the Nazis surrender? I'm just sayin'. Now, on to those sneaky little Japs. I'm gonna fuck them up real good. We've got something big cookin'. Get your popcorn ready. . . .

AUGUST 6, 1945

Just nuked the Japs. And if they keep talking shit, they're gonna get another one. I'm not even fucking around right now.

AUGUST 9, 1945

That's what happens when you talk shit, motherfucker! That's what happens! Just nuked Nagasaki. Maybe you should have thought through that Pearl Harbor thing and realized who you were fucking with. You were fucking with Harry S. Truman—the "S" stands for "Smoke my hog, you dirty little Japs!" OK, I think I've made my point. I'm done with the nukes. Well, maybe just one more . . . (JK!)

NOVEMBER 3, 1948

"Dewey Defeats Truman!" Good for Dewey! Oh no, wait. I'm just getting an update from the news desk—the new headline, "Dewey Sucks Truman's Balls!" Yep, I just won another term. Four more years of running shit. I'm thinking about nuking Korea. Also, coming out with a line of "The Buck Stops Here" merch. People dig that one.

DWIGHT D. EISENHOWER

JUNE 30, 1959

Winding down my run here. It went pretty well, I think. Honestly, I could have emptied the prisons and ordered the mass execution of puppies and it wouldn't matter. Once you

*have D-Day in your back pocket, you've got a pass for life.
People are like, "Mr. President, why aren't you doing more on
civil rights" and I shoot right back, "I'm sorry, I'm still a little
tired from DEFEATING THE NAZIS!" That's the
ultimate zinger!*

*My advice for the next guy? Keep an eye on those Commies!
And if you need me, just call 1-800-LOSE-THE-NUMBER.
I'll be playing golf and watching cartoons on the new TV thing.
Figure it out on your own.*

JOHN F. KENNEDY

OCTOBER 30, 1962

*Well, that sucked. Eisenhower was NOT kidding about the
Commies. Fuckers almost just launched missiles at us from
Cuba. Jesus. Bobby sweet-talked 'em out of it, thank God. I
haven't seen him that persuasive since the time he convinced
those twins into a four-way in Palm Beach! I swear he almost
had Khrushchev's pants off by the end of it.*

*Also, gotta give FDR a posthumous shout-out for putting
that pool in. Wow, am I slaying ass in that thing. And not
just the layup secretary ass. I'm flaunting internationally
famous movie stars inside the White House. I'm not going to
mention any names, but the one broad I'm nailing right now
has not left me with a "Seven Year Itch," thank goodness ;).
OK, it's Marilyn Monroe.*

Two things for the next guy:

1. *Stay the hell away from any place with the words "Bay" and "Pigs" in it.*

2. *I installed a secret tunnel under the East Wing that's good for escaping nuclear attack and smuggling whores. It's all yours.*

LYNDON B. JOHNSON

NOVEMBER 23, 1963

Thanks, Lee Harvey, you little shit. Now I'm president and all the wackos are gonna blame me, the Cubans, the mob, the CIA, space aliens, and everybody else. I did not have a central planning role. I only authorized it.

APRIL 1, 1968

I'm not much for writing in these queer journals, but I did just announce I'm not running for reelection. Should have quit while I was ahead on civil rights. I really fucked up this Vietnam thing. Who knew those little slopes could fight like that? I'm sure it'll be over soon and we'll learn our lesson forever about preemptive war. Not my problem anymore though. I'm outta here. Peace!

RICHARD M. NIXON

APRIL 17, 1973

I don't know why this book is here. I ordered all printed materials shredded and incinerated months ago. Just coverin' the ol' bases until this silly Watergate thing blows over. Can you believe all the hullabaloo? Those pranksters were just having some fun with the Democrats—a little gag among friends. "Break-in" has such a negative, criminal connotation. The Washington Post *has a big hard-on for the story, but luckily no one else gives a shit. You really think they're gonna turn over the country to Jerry Ford? Jesus Christ. That guy can't make it down a flight of stairs without falling on his face. You make that clown president and the Soviet tanks will be in Times Square by sundown.*

I just thank God no one knows about my secret tape recording system in this joint! I just figured it would be cool to have everything on tape for posterity. I'll probably make a cool mix tape of my "greatest hits" after I leave office as a national hero.

AUGUST 8, 1974

I have to resign over this bullshit? It's a goddamned attempted burglary, people! Did I jaywalk, too? Did I chew with my mouth full? Jesus Christ. Am I crazy here, guys? Tell me if I'm crazy. You'd think I was Mussolini the way they ran me out of office for a bunch of guys who aren't me breaking into an office. You want to blame me for the Lindbergh kidnapping, too? What am I missing?

Let's see the big fuckin' picture here, you assholes. I chilled China the fuck out and got us out of Vietnam and I'm leaving office in disgrace because a couple of copyboys at The Washington Post *decided a chickenshit burglary is a national story?*

I give up. This country is going to hell. You goddamned people don't deserve me. Have fun with Jerry.

GERALD R. FORD
AUGUST 10, 1974

Are you serious?! Are . . . you . . . serious?! A year ago I was arguing on the House floor to get funding for a new children's wing at the Grand Rapids Library and now I'm PRESIDENT?! President of the United States! Holy Christ! The Agnew thing was bad enough. This is a disaster, you guys. A few years back, LBJ said I was so dumb I "couldn't fart and chew gum at the same time." He's right! That is literally true. I've tried. I've got the chewing gum down and I've got the farts coming fast and furious, but just can't put the whole thing together.

How can I make sure this president thing doesn't last very long? I know! I'll pardon Nixon! Pretend none of that crap ever happened. I need to go write that down. Let's just hope the Democrats come up with a strong, impressive candidate and not some goober peanut farmer.

JIMMY CARTER
JULY 28, 1980

What do you want from me? Do you want me to just say it? OK, I suck. There you go. You happy? I'm a horrible,

*horrible president. I can't decide which part of my presidency
I'm more proud of: the hostages in Iran, the lines at gas
stations, or the fact that I was attacked by a "killer rabbit"
while I was on vacation in Plains. Jesus, that was an em-
barrassing four years. Hey, at least I kept the temperature
low in the White House, right? To the next guy: just don't do
stupid shit like that and you'll look brilliant by comparison.
Nowhere to go but up after this disaster. "Malaise" was an
understatement. You would almost need a movie star, like a
borderline fictional character, to ride in on a horse at this point
to rescue the country from my presidency. Again, I'm terribly
sorry.*

RONALD REAGAN

APRIL 7, 1981

*Wow, was it something I said? Some joker took a shot at me
last week. And I thought working with Bette Davis was
tough! This job seems like a pain in the ass already.*

JUNE 12, 1987

*Kind of a light day today, other than the part where I brought
about the end of the Cold War! Oh, man, you should have
heard the line I got off at the Berlin Wall. Ready? "Mr.
Gorbachev, tear down this wall!" My best work since the
underrated* Cattle Queen of Montana—*Barbara Stanwyck
at her very best. What was I talking about? Oh yeah, I ended
the Cold War today. Game over.*

AUGUST 11, 1988

The last eight years have been such a whirlwind I can hardly remember them. It's hard to choose just a small handful of my proudest achievements. I guess I'd say beating the Japs, giving women the vote, and freeing the slaves. Not a bad legacy when you see it all in front of you like that.

To my successor, whoever that may be, I offer you one solemn challenge. It's an undertaking that will seem to some impossible, even foolhardy. It may exceed the present bounds of human imagination. But I believe it to be our mission as presidents to always push the limits of possibility. That is why I declare to you here and now, in no uncertain terms, that we must put a man on the moon by the end of your presidency. The sky, my dear friend, shall no longer be the limit for this great country.

All best, Ronnie

GEORGE H. W. BUSH

JANUARY 4, 1993

My advice? Don't tell anybody to read your lips about anything. Sweet fancy Moses! It turns out people remember a line like that. On the upside, I took care of Iraq over a long weekend, so we won't have to deal with that cesspool ever again. Just cross it right off the list, my friends.

Despite that victory and the awesome "Thousand Points of Light" thing I came up with, America decided it wanted some hillbilly from Arkansas to run the country. So it's one

*term and out for ol' George Bush. You've seen the last of my
family. There will be no more Bush. Good luck to all of you.*

*p.s.—George W., if you're reading this book, we talked about
this—you were not to run for president. Call me as soon as
you get this message. You are in big trouble, young man.*

WILLIAM J. CLINTON
NOVEMBER 13, 2000
*A little advice here from a two-term president many are already
calling "the Greatest to Ever Live, Including Lincoln and
FDR." That is a direct quote I heard recently at a dinner party
held in my honor. I've also been called "the First Black President." I'm awfully proud of that because obviously there won't
be an actual black president anytime soon. Can you imagine?*

*So here are three lessons I've learned in my historic 8 years
in office that I hope will help you as you try to escape the long
shadow of my legacy.*

1. *Don't pick the fat ones. They're desperate and they've got
   nothing to lose. You want a gal with a lot on the line. A
   married woman with kids is the way to go—if she squeals,
   she gets herself into trouble, too. It's counterintuitive, I
   know, but trust me. I've done the research.*

2. *If you're going to introduce a foreign object—a cigar, for
   example—don't use the good stuff. I wasted a hundred-*

dollar Cuban and you know what I got in return? Articles of impeachment. NOT worth it.

3. *Nothing against group sex (obviously), but if you're going to have an orgy in the White House do it anywhere but the China Room. Panetta and I were in there with a bunch of sweeties from the Greek embassy one night and we smashed up a bunch of Lady Bird Johnson's stuff. That ruffled some feathers. Try the Blue Room.*

And one favor to ask the next president: Please screw up so horribly over the course of your administration that you not only enhance my presidency in hindsight, but also make my wife's inevitable run for the presidency an easy one. As long as you suck, we've got a cakewalk to the White House and she'll get off my ass. Thanks in advance. I owe ya one!

GEORGE W. BUSH

DECEMBER 29, 2008

Yo, Barack! How's it hangin', my man? Pumped for you being the first black guy to be president. Good stuff. Don't tell that cranky old coot McCain, but I was rooting for you the whole time. You remind me of a guy by the name of Ruben Sierra who used to play for the Texas Rangers when I owned the team in that you are also a black guy. Do you know Ruben?

By the way, any way you can start early? I'm in a celebrity golf tournament in Dallas early next month. Would love to get out of here ASAP. Boxes are packed. Just sitting here watching bowl games. Let me know.

Well, I'm not gonna leave you with a whole lot of advice—you seem like a smart cat. Just a few things before I leave.

1. *You do NOT have to wait in line for movies. One Sunday afternoon I walked over to the AMC Loews Theater on Connecticut Ave. there and waited an hour to see* Torque *(that movie with Ice Cube and the kick-ass motorcycles) before the Secret Service tracked me down. There's an entire theater in the White House! No lines and free Sour Patch Kids! How sweet is that?*

2. *Not that you have to worry about it anymore, but just an FYI that Saddam Hussein is a liar. I called him in a funny voice I use whenever I prank call a radio station and asked him if he had weapons of mass destruction. He laughed one of those evil villain laughs and said, "Of course I do!" Bam! I had him nailed—and I told him as much on the phone that day. So we went into Iraq and, well, you know the rest. Point being, don't rely only on your funny prank call voice to gather intelligence.*

3. *This is the big one, but don't say where you heard it. He's gonna be so pissed if he finds out I told you this, but what the hell: Cheney's the real president! Surprise! I pretty much just congratulated sports teams when they came to the*

*White House and tended to the rose garden while Cheney
ran the show. You believe that shit?*

*Later, Barry! Look me up if you're ever in Texas (I have
sick courtside Mavs tickets).*

President Obama closes the leather book. As he goes to turn
out the light and walk back up to bed, he hears a whistle that
echoes up the dumbwaiter shaft. It's Cheney. "Hey, Barack-
Attack! You still up there, Chief?" Before the president can answer, Cheney shouts again. "If you are, I'm gonna go ahead and
order an air strike on Iran. I'm bored as shit down here. Just a
little heads-up for the prez. Oh, and could you chuck some ranch
dressing down the chute? Thanks, Obama-Rama!"

8

Cable News Cool: The Hip-Hop Glossary

★

Author's note: Some say the mainstream media is stodgy and out of touch. I say, here's the proof. The following is based loosely on an actual memo distributed widely at a major news organization. I've added several terms and some color for effect. I also have changed the news outlet's name to protect it from the public humiliation it probably deserves. I may need a job there someday. I also should point out that the original e-mail was sent out several years before the election of Barack Obama. I added that completely misleading context to make the whole thing even worse.

For the record, the memo did not come from my current employer. We're incredibly hip at NBC. Just ask Willard Scott.

----Original Message----
From: The Front Office
To: BNO (Big News Organization) Staff
Subject: Get So Fabulous—A Hip-Hop Glossary

Team,

With the election of Barack Obama as president, we as a news organization need to be mindful of the rise of African-American culture in general. It is incumbent upon us to speak the language of the country—even if it is frightening and confusing. That's why we have assembled this "Get So Fabulous Hip-Hop Glossary" for your reference.

Please use this as a guide to help all you homeys and honeys add a new flava to your scripts and on-screen graphics. It is critically important to note here that regardless of what you may hear in popular music, it is never appropriate to use the n-word casually. That's a big no-no these days. Otherwise, have at it. Or, as they say in the community, "Handle ya bizness, playa!"

Thanks,
The Front Office

all that (*adj*): Possessing a wealth of positive attributes. Often used in conjunction with a popular snack food: *She's all that and a bag of chips!*

around the way (*n*): Connoting one who is down to earth and understands local etiquette and customs, as in an "around the way girl" (in contrast with a "ho").

Audi 5000 (*interj*): Phrase one uses as one departs: *I'm outta here, I'm Audi 5000!* Unrelated to ownership of, or travel in, the popular Audi sedan of the same name.

baby mama (*n*): The mother of one's child, typically used to describe an unmarried parent. As you know, out-of-wedlock birth is a big problem for these folks, so let's be sensitive there.

baller (*n*): Ballplayer, though often used to denote one who has garnered a reputation for success (legitimate or criminal). Includes a connotation of success with the fairer sex (sometimes referred to as "bitches," "hos," or "tricks").

bank (*n*): Money. This is a tough one because it doesn't mean the place where the money is stored. It's just the money itself. I know, that makes no sense. Don't shoot the messenger. Keep an open mind. [See also *cheese, cheddar, benjamins,* and *dead presidents.*]

benjamins (*n*): Money, specifically $100 bills, as in P. Diddy's "It's All About the Benjamins." You see, Benjamin Franklin's face appears on a $100 bill.

bling (*n*): Jewelry, especially the large gold, platinum, and diamond rings and pendants favored by those sporting the "ghetto fabulous" style. An example is the "Jesus Piece" worn by Kanye West. Upper-middle-class white moms have started to use this one.

blow up the spot (*v*): To give a great performance onstage. Generally used to describe hip-hop artists, but let's broaden it out on the air: *Hey, Gary! Great report on the five-day weather outlook. You totally blew up the spot!* [Note: should not be used to punch up our Afghanistan or Iraq coverage.]

blunt (*n*): marijuana rolled into the shell of a Phillies Blunt cigar. [Note: marijuana is illegal and should not be glorified here at BNO.]

bounce (*v*): To depart, get going, move on. [Point of personal privilege here: also a terrific Gwyneth Paltrow/Ben Affleck vehicle a few years back. Grab the Kleenex!]

bug (*v*): To behave inappropriately, irrationally, or strangely: *Why you acting so crazy? You buggin'!* Not related in this context to insects.

catch the vapors (*v*): To be overly involved in, or covetous of, another's popularity, style, or vibe. [Note: our sources report that no one has said this for 20 years.]

chill 1. (*v*): An entreaty (or command) to relax. Also a smart thing to do with Chardonnay 20 minutes before company comes over. 2. (*adj*): Relaxed and mellow.

crib (*n*): A person's home. As the recent years of *MTV Cribs* has taught us, pretty much anything with a front door and a roof is considered a "crib." [Note: not considered "ghetto fabulous" when used to describe an infant's bed.]

Cristal (*n*): Expensive champagne often preferred by hip-hop artists and sprayed from VIP sections of nightclubs as a display of wealth.

dawg (*n*): Term of endearment to describe a friend: *That's my dawg right there!* or *I feel you, dawg!* You may recognize this usage from *American Idol* judge Randy Jackson, who, surprisingly, is not considered part of the hip-hop community. Go figure.

dis (*v*): To insult or disparage. Short for "disrespect": *Hey, you! Don't dis my new Sperry Top-Siders!*

dope (*adj*): Very good, high quality, fantastic. Also slang for "drugs," which have plagued urban communities for decades now. It's really sad, but what are you gonna do, right?

down with (*adv*): Embracing a particular idea, activity, or thing: *Are you down with that? You'd better believe I am! Wait, what are we talking about?*

drop science, drop knowledge (*v*): To provide wisdom or skill. To instruct. This one confuses me. The "knowledge" part I get. It's all the "dropping" I'm hung up on. I've asked our lawyers to check into it.

flava (*n*): Flavor, style: *Give it your own flava, yo.* Let's be honest, and we don't mean to be insensitive, but this one is just a flat-out misspelling of the word "flavor."

floss (*v*): To show off, most often with an overt display of material wealth. Flashing items (e.g., one's *cheddar* or *bling*) in the faces of others. Also, and I don't mean to be a nag here, something you really ought to do after every meal.

flow (*v*): To rhyme continuously: *Hey, Mr. Man! Chiggity check out my flow over here!*

fly (*adj*): Sexually attractive, lovely, or handsome. Different from "bug" for some reason.

forty (*n*): A forty-ounce container of beer, typically malt liquor like Olde English 800 or Colt 45. [Note: white people drink these only ironically.]

freak 1. (*v*): To have sex. 2. (*n*): Sexually aggressive female. Hip-hop artist Ludacris [*sic*] puts it in context when he raps, "We want a lady in the street, but a freak in the bed."

fresh (*adj*): New or of high quality. Same concept as produce at Whole Foods, but with sneakers and baggy clothing. [See also **dope**.]

front (*v*): To masquerade as something you are not: *Don't front, you're totally not a good canasta player!*

ghetto fabulous (*adj*): Over-the-top style. Think mink coat in the summertime. Not to be confused with the term "Fabulous!" That'll be in next week's staff memo: "Faaaaabuloussssss!—Understanding the Gays."

grill (*n*): One's personal space: *Why you all up in my grill?* Literally, one's teeth or the diamond caps placed over the original teeth. Often seen in its plural form "grillz." Really excessive, if I may say. They should put that money into a Roth IRA.

hardcore (*adj*): Authentic or extreme. Also, the only kind of porn there is, if you ask me.

holla (*v*): To get in touch with someone, as in: *Holla at me, playa!* Helpful hint: pronounced just like "challah," the delicious braided bread served at Sabbath meals.

homeboy/homegirl (*n*): A close friend. You've definitely heard this one. Come on.

homey (*n*): See **homeboy**.

honey (*n*): An attractive female.

hood (*n*): Neighborhood, community. Used earnestly in urban culture and ironically in suburban slang, as in: *'He's cool—he's from the 'hood back in Greenwich.'*

Hova (*n*): Self-ascribed nickname for popular rapper Jay-Z. An abbreviation of Jehovah, or God. They're a very brazen people.

hype (*n*): Positive, laudatory information about a person or thing, often premature or inaccurate: *Don't believe the hype!* (Also a song from the rap group Public Enemy that scared the poop out of white people several years back.)

ice (*n*): Diamonds or diamond jewelry: *Look at her floss with all that ice, dawg/homey.*

ill (*v*): To behave inappropriately, obnoxiously, or weirdly: *Stop illin'!* Conversely, ill may also be used as an adjectival superlative: *Man, that single was ill!* May also be used to describe physical sickness, but, again, that would not be deemed "ghetto fabulous."

in the house (*n*): The state of being present, on the premises. [Also *in the heezie, in da building.*]

Jacob the Jeweler (*n*): New York City jeweler Jacob Arabo, preferred by the hip-hop and professional sports communities. Featured in many rap songs and in several indictments.

krunk (*adj*): used to describe an exceptionally good time, usually involving alcohol: *Say, Richard, this corporate retreat is totally krunk!*

make it rain (*v*): To shower a group of people with paper currency, typically at a strip club. The larger the playa, the larger the amount of cash used to create said rain. The smaller playas rush to collect the money they've just thrown.

off the hook (*adj*): Excellent, fun, rad. [Also *off the chain* and *off the heezie, for sheezie.*]

old school (*adj*): Describes something that inspires nostalgia from a previous era. *Dang it, Steve! Those Stan Smith tennis shoes are old school!*

paper (*n*): Currency, and not just that of the United States. Euros have come into favor with the hip-hop elite due to the recent slide of the dollar.

peeps (*n*): People. Often refers to one's cronies, community, or family. Also a delicious Easter treat that can be enjoyed all year round.

phat (*adj*): The best, terrific, extremely *dope* and *fresh*. This is a delicate one. Use it incorrectly and we have a lawsuit from a fat person on our hands. Get approval from your direct manager before going with this.

play yourself (*v*): To reveal vulnerability, to make a fool of yourself. [Important note: different than playing *with* oneself.]

played out (*adj*): Archaic, no longer hip: *Excuse me, sir! That Volvo wagon is played out. Why don't you get a Peugeot or something while you're at it!* (Ha! Burn!)

player (*n*): Typically refers to playboy types, those skilled at collecting digits from the honeys. Pronounced "play-ah" (the mispronunciation of these terms is critical to the success of their use).

player haters (*n*): Those who disparage high rollers and players, usually because they are unsuccessful or unable to be players themselves. [Note: I once heard someone say on TV, *Don't hate the player, hate the game!* I don't know what that means, but give it a shot!]

posse (*n*): One's coterie or clan. The group of people one surrounds oneself with. [Note: using the word "coterie" is generally a good way to get your ass kicked.]

represent (*v*): To demonstrate pride in or bring honor to one's local community. *I'm representin' Westchester County, ya heard?!*

ride (*n*): Car, typically a leased sports car or large SUV with televisions in the headrests.

rims (*n*): Custom-made exposed portion of tires, usually silver and often costing more than the ride whose wheels they cover.

roll (*v*): To congregate or travel with a particular group or person: *Let's roll to Brooks Brothers to cop some of those phat noniron dress shirts!*

shorty (*n*): Little person or kid. Most often means an attractive female. [Note: not to be used to describe a "little person" in the technical sense—they're very touchy and ornery.]

slamming (*adj*): Fantastic, really good or extremely attractive, stylin'. [Note: have some fun with this one, gang, and drop the "g"—as in "slammin'"! [See also **phat**.]

sucka (*n*): One who is easily fooled or manipulated. [Note: to better understand our African-American audience, rent *I'm Gonna Git You Sucka*. A spot-on depiction.]

sweat (*v*): To harass, bother, or worry: *Stop sweating on me! It's totally gross! Yuck!*

tight (*adj*): Everything's going well, all's in its place, feeling good, as it should be—like a good pair of pleated khakis.

trip (*v*): To overreact or act irrationally: *Hey, don't trip over that extension cord, playa!*

wack (*adj*): Bad, detrimental: *Yo! This Hip-Hop Glossary is the opposite of wack! As a matter of fact, it's fresh and totally krunk! The management at BNO just made it rain with knowledge, suckas! We're currently Audi 5000! (The slang meaning—we're not leaving in an Audi sedan.)*

TRUE STORY . . .

"I AM THEM"
Woman calls 911 to report own drunk driving

The ethics of drunk driving are pretty clear-cut. Contrary to what your old man says, booze does not "help you focus" while driving (that only works for bowling and billiards). But what would a freshman ethics student do with the case of the forty-nine-year-old Wisconsin woman who called 911 to notify police that there was someone out on the road driving under the influence, and that someone was her?

The driver had knocked down "7 or 8 brandy and Cokes" at various bars around Neillsville, Wisconsin, before she got behind the wheel to head home. Apparently that journey was not going well, so the woman took it upon herself to call 911 about a drunk driver on the road. Here's how the exchange with the emergency operator went from there:

> *Dispatch: You behind them?*
> *Drunk Lady: No, I am them.*
> *Dispatch: You am them?*
> *Drunk Lady: Yes, I am them.*
> *Dispatch: Okay, so you want to call and report you're driving drunk?*
> *Drunk Lady: Yes.*
> *Dispatch: Are you still driving right now? You want to stop driving before you get in an accident.*
> *Drunk Lady: Yes, I will stop.*

The Drunk Lady pulled over and waited for police to arrive. She failed field sobriety tests miserably before telling the officers about the brandy and Cokes. She blew a healthy .17 and was arrested for drunk driving.

Yes, driving drunk is objectively bad—no two ways about it. But do we as a society ignore the good deed that followed? Does it count for nothing? Do we throw the sinner out of the church for good?

Or do we reward her brave decision to right the wrong? Whatever happened to redemption? Can you imagine if we had left Ted Kennedy on the ash heap of history after his traffic troubles? Perhaps Drunk Lady will also go on to become one of our greatest United States senators. Who can say for sure?

Ethicists, and drunk drivers, will debate these important questions for generations to come.

7

The Bachelorette: A Vote for Love

★

One beautiful woman looking for the man of her dreams. Twenty-five creepy politicians vying for her heart. This is . . . The Bachelorette: A Vote for Love.

I'm your host Chris Harrison and this is the season finale of *The Bachelorette: A Vote for Love.* Tonight, after 12 weeks of laughter, tears, and unforgettable rose ceremonies, Heather will make the most difficult decision of her life: which of the two remaining political creeps will she choose—and which will be sent home heartbroken like 23 men before him? Before we hand out the final rose, let's go all the way back to Day One to hear why our bachelorette came here looking for love.

"My name is Heather, I'm a 27-year-old technical business relations consultant from Lake Oswego, Oregon. I've been in some really bad relationships, so I'm definitely here to fall in love and find someone to share my life with. My grandmother always told me that the best way to find a meaningful relationship is to become a contestant on a reality television show. So here I am, Nana.

"I guess I'd say I'm attracted to powerful men. Especially elected officials with complicated private lives and deviant sexual habits. My last relationship was with a member of the Lake Oswego City Council. We broke up after he was fired for downloading Malaysian scat porn on a government computer. It broke my heart to lose him that way.

"I'm hoping and believing that one of these 25 amazing men is the One. I'm looking for love. If I don't find it here, I don't think I'll find it anywhere."

Let's bring her out on the biggest night of her life—ladies and gentlemen, say hello to Heather. You look absolutely stunning. How are you feeling?

"Wow. Honestly, I feel sick to my stomach. This is the hardest thing I've ever had to do. No one prepares you for the fact that you can fall in love with two different creeps at the same time. My night in the Ikea Fantasy Suite with Governor Spitzer only made this harder. Ugh. I'm so confused right now, Chris."

There is no question you have a very difficult decision to make. Two successful, freaky politicians, and only one rose. This promises to be our most dramatic rose ceremony ever. I know I'm contractually obligated to say that every week, but this really is huge.

Heather, before you make that choice, the guys made one final pitch for your heart. They asked me to pass along these personal video messages. The first one is from Mark, and brought to you by Buffalo Wild Wings.

MARK, 50
South Carolina Governor

Hey, Heather. I can't believe this is all ending. What a magical journey. I don't even want to think about the possibility of not being with you when this is over. I thought I had found my soulmate in that Argentine lady until I met you. Plus, the commute to Buenos Aires was becoming a real bitch. So you are my soulmate, Heather. A lot of guys would be afraid to use a douchey term like "soulmate" in public, but Mark Sanford doesn't care what anybody thinks. You are my soulmate. Soulmate, soulmate, soulmate!

Of course my first reaction when I saw you was, Wow! She's super-hot. God's telling me not to do it, but my heart, and my dong, disagree with the Man Upstairs on this one. I'll admit, I hoped you'd get a chance to see that dong I just mentioned because when I go tanning, I brown the whole bird. Also, I thought, she's really gonna get along great with my four boys. This person could be my soulmate, and she's got great haunches for hiking.

But it wasn't until our group date that I truly fell in love. The moment you grabbed my hand and kissed me while we all were out deep sea fishing is one I'll cherish forever. I felt bad for Gary Hart just sitting there awkwardly and for my friend John Ensign hurling over the side of the boat, because they're both super-cool guys, but for those few magical seconds, there were only two people on that vessel: Mark and Heather. "Magical" is a pretty douchey word, too, I guess, but if telling you that you are my "magical soulmate" makes me a douche bag, then I guess I'm a complete douche bag.

As I've told you, Heather, I will move to Oregon with you in a heartbeat. My term as governor is up and here's a news flash: Columbia, South Carolina, is a hellhole. I love God, but I'm afraid he forgot to shine his light on Columbia. Good Lord, is it bad. The farther and faster I can get away from there, the better. Plus, I need to get away from my ex-wife. She scares the s**t out of me. That woman is a Lifetime movie waiting to happen. You'd fake long trips on the Appalachian Trail, too, trust me. She's terrifying. I don't mean to be presumptuous, but I have my bags packed already. If you screw me over here tonight, I'll probably just go stay on my buddy's couch in Myrtle Beach 'til this thing blows over.

Before I go, I just want to leave you with one of my all-time favorite quotes. It comes from Dr. Meredith Grey on *Grey's Anatomy*. She said to McDreamy, "Pick me. Choose me. Love me." So I ask you, Heather, to pick me, to choose me, and to love me. Oh, man. I hate that I'm crying right now. I should probably tell you up front that I might do something drastic if you don't pick me—I'm in a weird place right now. Just an FYI. Love you, doll. You are my soulmate.

Powerful stuff, Heather. How you feeling after seeing that?

"Well, he's definitely a giant pussy—what man quotes *Grey's Anatomy* and uses the word 'soulmate' that liberally? Sometimes I wonder if he's gay. But there's something very endearing about him. Kind of a dim-witted Southern charm. His is a unique brand of creepiness."

No question about it. A lot to think about there, but right now let's turn to the other man fighting for your affection tonight. This personal video message comes to you from Eliot, and the good people at Listerine Breath Strips.

ELIOT, 51

Former New York Governor

What's up, Heather, you tasty little tomcat? It's me, Grendel. Grrrrrrrr! Sorry, America—little inside joke there. I'm gonna be honest with you, Heather, I didn't come here looking for love. Some of my advisors thought it would be a good move for the ol' career rehab. That Client 9 business set me back a bit. The idea was that I'd look to the public like a man who knew how to love and respect women and not just a creep who likes to have hookers step on him with stilettos while he's tied to a medieval torture rack. I just liked the idea because I figured there'd be some primo twenty-something ass involved.

Well, a funny thing happened on the way to career rehab— I fell head-over-heels for a nice little slut named Heather who doesn't mind dressing up like Princess Leia for "the Luv Guv." I trademarked "Luv Guv" by the way—full line of energy bars and crotchless panties on my Web site. Little plug there.

So when did I know this was something special? I guess it was that first night when we were in the hot tub with former Florida congressman Mark Foley—thank God you unloaded that freak, by the way. He didn't seem terribly interested in you as he chugged champagne alone while sitting directly on the high-pressure jets, so I made my move. Even by my standards, we got pretty kooky that night (hint: Ping Pong balls plus instant gravy equals fun). But I knew you were a different kind of broad when I pulled out my money to pay for our night together. You pushed my hand away and said, "You don't have to pay. I'm not a prostitute." Do you remember what I said, Heather? I said, "Really? You could have fooled me with that gymnastics routine. I didn't know whether to bang you or give you a perfect ten." We shared a good laugh over that and then I said, "But wait, seriously, this one's free?" I feel like that was a big moment for us.

From there, things only got more amazing. I don't kiss and tell, but let's just say our one-on-one date in a hot air balloon definitely broke some FAA regulations. Ah, screw it, I'll just say it: Heather stuffed an apple in my mouth like I was a holiday pig, hit me over the head with a sandbag, and sodomized me with a zucchini. Whatever happens tonight, we'll always have that day. No one can take that away from us.

Then there were the little things that really started to add up. We realized that we both love, love, love Michael Bublé, we both keep vegetable peelers in our bedside tables (what are

the odds?!), and we share the same safe word ("Beowulf!").
When you screamed that at the top of your lungs on that fate-
ful night, I realized that some greater force of destiny had put
us in that steam shower together.

So here's the deal. I've had fun, you've had fun. If you want
to take this thing to the next level, I've got some ideas. What if
we hijacked a plane and had sex in the cockpit before turning
the aircraft back over to the crew peacefully? I've always had
a hijacking fantasy. Just throwing it out there. Heather, I
know this sounds corny, but I don't want to hijack a commercial jet and have sex in the cockpit with anyone but you.

So pick the right guy. Do you really think that other hick
is going to give you the marathon humiliation sessions you
ache for? Let's get weird.

Wow. Heather, you're crying. Why?

"I can't do this, Chris. It's too hard. This isn't fair. I wasn't
totally sure Governor Spitzer was here for the right reasons, and
now I know he is. He wants to hijack a plane and have sex with
me in the cockpit. I wish my grandmother was still alive to hear
that."

I know how tough this seems, Heather. It feels like a big deal
right now, but, honestly, these relationships don't last, so don't
get too worked up about the decision. Our success rate on this
show is like 8 percent. The over/under on you and the guy you
choose here is 3 months and most of the guys on the crew here
are taking the under. I don't mean to undermine the entire prem-
ise of the show, but you really could just flip a coin.

"Chris, I feel very deeply for these two men. Please respect that."

Okay. I'll remind you of that deep love in 3 months when you're living alone in Studio City auditioning for cat food commercials. Let's get on with it, Heather. The decision is yours. Will it be Mark or Eliot? Two creeps, one rose. Gentlemen, come on out.

"Thanks, Chris . . . I think. God, my heart is pounding out of my chest. We started this journey with 25 of the creepiest, sex-freak politicians in the country and I honestly believe I have the two creepiest of all standing in front of me. Just think, you were both considered stars in your political parties. I mean, Jesus, Mark, they wanted you to run for president. And look at you now.

"I have come to love you both over the last couple of months in different ways. Mark, you are a beautiful romantic. Eliot, you are a demented sadomasochist. I've learned so much from you two disgraced politicians. Mark, your tedious stories about outdoor adventure taught me patience. Eliot, your floggings taught me how to enjoy pain. I want to thank you both with all of my heart.

"This is the toughest decision I've had to make since Eliot made me choose between the gimp mask and the horse bit in the Ikea Fantasy Suite the other night. Or when Mark made me contemplate a choice between jumping out the window or stabbing myself in the neck with a letter opener when he started talking about being my soulmate again. What a pussy.

"As hard as it's been, I've made my decision. Ahhhh, I can't do this."

Take your time, Heather. We'll drop in some of that super-dramatic piano music in postproduction to fill the silence. Whenever you're ready, you may choose the man with whom you will spend at least the next month of your life.

"OK, I'm fine. Deep breath. Do it for Nana. All right, here goes: Eliot . . . will you accept this rose?"

"Are you serious?"

"Yes, Eliot, I am. Will you accept this rose and love me forever?"

"Whoa, whoa, whoa! Slow down there. What's the safe word again? Beowulf! I want out! You really thought I came on a TV show to find a girlfriend? Puh-lease! I've got enough problems. I don't need some stalker wannabe-actress, reality TV contestant in my life. This was just sex, honey. Plain and simple. Mark, she's all yours there, Latin lover boy. Take her up in a hot air balloon. It'll blow your mind. I'm out."

Wow, this is uncomfortable. Heather, would you like to give the rose to Mark instead? You have that option under the official *Bachelorette* rules agreed upon at the Geneva Conventions.

"No, actually. I'm gonna run, too. My laundry's been piling up. Plus, Mark is a douche."

Sorry, Mark. Looks like it's back to search the long Appalachian Trail of love for you. Please gather your things and leave.

Well, historians will most certainly look back at this finale as the most shocking and dramatic in *Bachelorette* history. Please join us in the fall for an all-new season of *The Bachelor,* when we finally just cut the pretense and round up a bunch of strippers, put them in bikinis, pump them full of pills and vodka, and let them wrestle in tapioca pudding for the heart of a single dad. Good night, everyone!

8

Blago: The Raw, Unedited FBI Tapes

★

The federal corruption trial of former Illinois governor Rod Blagojevich will be remembered best, perhaps, for the defendant's rollicking courtroom performance of Elvis Presley's "Return to Sender" during his closing argument, after which Mr. Blagojevich memorably pointed to the jury and shouted, "I dare you to convict the King!" In another attempt to win over the 12 people who would decide his legal fate, the defendant later brandished a pressurized T-shirt gun and attempted to fire FREE BLAGO! shirts into the jury box. A bailiff tackled him before he could get off a shot. After the incident, Mr. Blagojevich was forced to wear a Hannibal Lecter–like restraint for the remainder of the trial.

The outbursts only served to underscore the circuslike nature of the proceedings inside the United States District Court in Chicago. The tone for the trial was set early on by the release of a series of transcripts of the FBI's months-long wiretap surveillance of a telephone belonging to Mr. Blagojevich. Although the recorded calls were, in most cases, not relevant to the charges at hand, attorneys for the former governor said after the trial that the pattern of behavior they revealed proved "not helpful" to their defense.

Herewith are selected transcripts of FBI intercepts of telephone communications between Mr. Rod Blagojevich and a number of persons who, it must be pointed out, have not been charged with any criminal wrongdoing.

FEDERAL BUREAU OF INVESTIGATION
JULY 17, 2008

SPEAKERS:
BLAGO: Illinois governor Rod Blagojevich
BOBBY: Robert Simmons, Little Caesars Pizza employee

BLAGO: Look, Bobby, we can work something out here. I'm sure you don't want to be working behind that counter and wearing that f**kin' headset forever.

BOBBY: Sir, I have to charge you for the Crazy Bread. I'd be happy to give you some of our signature Crazy Sauce compliments of the house.

BLAGO: How'd you like to run the Chicago Department of Sanitation? That's one phone call, Bobby. Just throw in the goddamned Crazy Bread. Do the right thing here, kid.

BOBBY: The Department of Sanitation? I'm not sure who this is, but I really can't give out the Crazy Bread for free. I have other customers waiting, sir. Do you want the pizza or not?

BLAGO: This is your motherf**kin' governor, you smarmy little c***sucker. Do you have any idea who you're f**kin' with here? You're in way over your f**kin' head. How'd you like to have the National Guard kickin' down your f**kin' door tonight, you little f**k? That can happen, too.

BOBBY: So should I cancel the order of Crazy Bread, sir? Just the large Hula Hawaiian pizza then?

BLAGO: F**k you! Just send over the motherf**kin' pizza. You made a big mistake here today, Bobby.

BOBBY: OK, sir. Your total is $15.99. We'll see you in about 30 minutes.

FEDERAL BUREAU OF INVESTIGATION
SEPTEMBER 14, 2008

SPEAKERS:
BLAGO: Illinois governor Rod Blagojevich
JANICE: Janice St. Jean, Home Shopping Network operator

BLAGO: Well, Janice, that's a shame because I gotta tell you I really had my heart set on those bed linens from the Priscilla Presley Collection. You seem like an awfully sweet gal—maybe there's an arrangement to be made here.

JANICE: I'm not sure I understand. As I said, we're completely out of stock on the Priscilla Presley Collection. That's been a big seller for us. Could I suggest some ballerina flats from Isaac Mizrahi's new line, exclusive to us here at HSN?

BLAGO: Janice, it's just your luck you answered a call from a guy who's not gonna take no for an answer. [Laughter from BLAGO.] You've got something I want. Perhaps I have something you want, too.

JANICE: What? Sir, I . . .

BLAGO: I'll just lay it out for you, Janice: my state lottery commissioner is a piece of sh*t. That stays between you, me, and the wall, but it's the f**kin' truth. How'd you like to run the Illinois state lottery, effective immediately? Do you really think anyone notices when a couple of bucks go missing from that giant lottery pot? Trust me, Janice: I'm not looking. [More laughter from BLAGO.]

JANICE: Who is this? What's happening? I should probably terminate this call. . . .

BLAGO: Okay, I get it—you'd rather answer the f**king phone at the Home Shopping Network than hold a powerful government position.

Well, I'm gonna spell this out real nice and simple for ya, Janice: if I don't have the f**kin' Priscilla Presley pillow shams by the end of this motherf**kin' phone call, we're gonna have a problem that goes way above your f**kin' pay grade. You got me?

JANICE: Sir, I'm sorry you're upset, but we do not tolerate that kind of verbal abuse from customers. I'm going to hang up—

BLAGO: F**k you, Janice! And tell that f**kin' queer Mizrahi not to float away in those f**kin' ballerina flats!

FEDERAL BUREAU OF INVESTIGATION
OCTOBER 21, 2008

SPEAKERS:
BLAGO: Illinois governor Rod Blagojevich
ROB: Rob Blagojevich, the governor's brother and chairman of Friends of Blagojevich

BLAGO: It looks like Obama's gonna win this f**kin' thing. You believe that sh*t? What a f**kin' joke. That should have been me, Rob. That should have been me. F**k me in the hairy Serbian ass!

ROB: That guy is a motherf**kin' clown. We wouldn't have taken a meeting with him a couple years ago and now he's gonna be f**kin' president of the United States? Go f**kin' figure. We'll run against that f**ker in four years and we'll beat his ass, too, Rod.

BLAGO: Hey, Rob, why the f**k did our f**kin' mom give us names only one letter off from each other? It's a f**kin' pain in the ass. I never know if you're asking me a f**kin' question or just talkin' to your f**kin' self again. [Laughter from BLAGO and ROB.] And it's gonna be a hell of a f**kin' kick in the balls to the FBI if they ever have to transcribe a wiretap call between us! [Laughter from BLAGO.] A f**kin' "Who's on First" routine over here! [Laughter from ROB.] Can you imagine that sh*t?

ROB: [Laughter from ROB.] Lucky for us, those douche bag feds are too f**kin' dumb to catch on ... Rod.

BLAGO: [Hysterical laughter from BLAGO.] Wait, wait, get your pencils ready, sh*t-for-brains FBI—did you say "Rod"? Or "Rob"? [Laughter from BLAGO and ROB.] Oh, this is great sh*t, bro. How great would it be if they really were listening to this sh*t? Too f**kin' bad.

ROB: [More laughter from BLAGO and ROB.] So when Obama or Osama or whatever the f**k his name is gets elected, what are we gonna get for his f**kin' Senate seat? I want a f**kin' pontoon boat, Rod. I really want one of those motherf**kers. Ever partied on a pontoon boat? It's like you're floating on the f**kin' water!

BLAGO: Way ahead of you. I threw that motherf**ker's seat on Craigslist weeks ago just to get a feel for the demand. Let me tell you, this thing is f**kin' golden.

ROB: F**k yeah! This is like f**kin' Christmas!

BLAGO: I might give that sh*t to Oprah! Who the f**k has more money than that b*tch?! Look what she did for that chubby little no-talent Rachael Ray. Hey, Oprah: how about a f**kin' talk show for Rockin' Rod over here?! [*Conversation interrupted by the apparent sound of running water.*]

ROB: Are you taking a piss, Rod?

BLAGO: Yeah, sorry, dude. [*The toilet flushes.* BLAGO *fart, groan, and unintelligible comment.*]

ROB: Jesus Christ, man.

BLAGO: [BLAGO *fart again.*] Somebody stepped on a duck in here, Rob. Classic Dangerfield line, right?

ROB: [Laughter from ROB.] F**kin' classic.

BLAGO: So let's work up a list of sh*t we want and then get it out to the right people on this thing right away.

ROB: Yep.

BLAGO: So far I've offered the seat to that a**hole who runs the steakhouse we like over on Rush Street. Can you say "garlic mashed potatoes for life"? He'd owe us big time.

ROB: He'd be f**kin' great, and so would those f**kin' mashed potatoes.

BLAGO: And Patti's been buggin' me to get her a Sebring forever, so I offered it to some c***sucker over at the Chrysler dealership in Schaumburg. You shoulda seen the look on this f**kin' guy's face when I asked him if he wanted to be a United States senator. He gave us a loaner while he sleeps on it. That Sebring is surprisingly roomy for a convertible, by the way.

ROB: Yeah, they're f**kin' nice.

BLAGO: And then, let's see—oh, I offered the seat to the Milwaukee Bucks for Michael Redd and a first-round draft pick. That f**kin' kid can shoot and God knows the horsesh*t Bulls could use him.

ROB: F**kin' golden, Hot Rod! But tell the Bucks to throw in a pontoon boat, those cheap f**ks.

[BLAGO *speaks away from the receiver to an unidentified woman.*]

BLAGO: What's that, honey? Oh, okay. [BLAGO *speaks into the receiver again.*] Yeah, Rob, that's Patti, she's got a real quick message for you: go f**k yourself, you big, dumb f**kin' oaf.

ROB: [laughing] I'd tell her to go f**k herself, but knowing your complete f**kin' impotence, I have a feeling she's already doing plenty of that, you dumb f**ks.

BLAGO: [laughing] Ah, f**k you. All right, gotta run, Rob. I'll let you know what I hear.

ROB: Sounds good, Rod. F**k you.

BLAGO: OK, f**k you, too, buddy.

FEDERAL BUREAU OF INVESTIGATION
DECEMBER 8, 2008

SPEAKERS:
BLAGO: Illinois governor Rod Blagojevich
WRONG NUMBER: Unknown female caller

BLAGO: This is Rod.

WRONG NUMBER: Um, is Cheryl there?

BLAGO: Who the f**k is Cheryl?

WRONG NUMBER: I'm sorry. I think I have the wrong number.

BLAGO: I think you do. Call here again and a wrong number will be the least of your f**kin' problems.

WRONG NUMBER: Good-bye.

BLAGO: Wait, how'd you like to be the next senator from the great state of Illinois?

[*Dial tone.*]

BLAGO: F**k you.

TRUE STORY . . .

WHEN A MAN MEETS A COIN-OPERATED VACUUM . . .
Area man caught having sex with car wash vacuum

Far be it from me to judge the sexual eccentricities of another man, but from where I'm sitting, screwing a coin-operated car wash vacuum cleaner seems a bit, well, desperate. A 29-year-old man was arrested in Thomas Township, Michigan, after police received a call reporting "suspicious activity" at the Marathon Fill and Wash.

The responding officer wisely parked his cruiser a safe distance from an automobile that had the hose from a humming stationary vacuum cleaner snaked into the driver's side window. Approaching on foot, the officer immediately upgraded the activity he observed from "suspicious" to the more specific law enforcement term "Jesus Christ, man! What the f**k are you doing?"

The suspect had his pants down, guiding the industrial-strength vacuum hose toward his crotch with one hand and holding a roll of quarters in the other. One assumes Whitesnake was playing on the radio. Without even a hint of the common courtesy to let the man finish the moment of intimacy for which he plainly had paid his good money, the officer moved in for the arrest. Total cock block.

The man pleaded guilty to indecent exposure, which is lawyer speak for "getting a hummer from a public vacuum cleaner." He was sentenced to 90 days in jail by yet another activist judge imposing his outdated concept of morality from the bench. It turns out, even in the year 2010, institutionalized discrimination is alive and well in the supposed "land of the free."

9

The Longest Yard:
Guantánamo Bay

★

LATE TURNOVER SCUTTLES DETAINEES' COMEBACK BID FOR FREEDOM

ESPN.com wire services

U.S. NAVAL STATION GUANTÁNAMO BAY, Cuba—For a group of prisoners long in search of justice, there was none on the final drive of Saturday's decisive game between this detention facility's enemy combatants and the members of the U.S. Military Police who guard them.

Quarterback and Pakistani militant Muhammad Arsha Raza led the upstart Fightin' Detainees into scoring position with a dramatic 83-yard drive in the game's final 1:45 that called to mind the clutch performances of John Elway and Joe Montana, and made some forget for a moment Raza's foiled plots to attack Western embassies and behead foreign diplomats across the Middle East.

But on the doorstep of a monumental upset, with freedom just three short yards and 19 seconds away, swivel-hipped running back Haji Mohammed Khan, the Afghan fighter accused in a botched attempt to drive a truck full of ammonium nitrate into a library to prevent women and girls from reading, took a handoff from Raza, darted to his left, and, without being hit by a defender, mysteriously lost control of the ball. American MPs pounced, recovering the fumble and sealing a hard-fought 31–28 victory for the Americans.

Many of the enemy combatants collapsed on the field in disbelief as they watched their guards celebrate a United States win whose impact was felt around the globe. A fatwa was issued on Khan effective immediately after the game.

"I never had a good handle on the ball," said Khan in the losing locker room. "I let my fellow suspected terrorists down. What can you say at a time like this, except, you know, death to America."

The football game billed as "The Battle on the Bay" drew the eyes of the world after it was announced by the United States Justice Department early this year as the official means by which the fate of prisoners held at U.S. Naval Station Guantánamo Bay would be decided. Attorney General Eric Holder was quoted at the time as saying, "We've been going back and forth on what to do with these people for years. To be perfectly honest, we just plumb ran out of ideas. So we're gonna do this *Longest Yard*–style: inmates versus guards. Detainees win, they're free to go. Guards win, we hang on to the terrorists for a while. Excuse me, 'suspected' terrorists. Whatever."

Amnesty International and the ACLU, among many other groups, have decried the Justice Department's decision to settle the hotly debated question of the handling of detainees at Guantánamo Bay with a game of American-style football.

"Are you shitting me?" an ACLU spokesman said last month in a statement. "Many of these victims have been held at Guantánamo for nearly a decade without any charge at all. And now, instead of giving them lawyers, we're giving them a football game to win their freedom? This is an outrage and yet another blow to America's reputation around the world.

"At a minimum we would like a more international sport, like soccer, to be used, in the interest of fairness, as the determining competition. Or better yet, buzkashi, the traditional Central Asian game where players on horseback pick up the headless carcass of a goat and carry it across a goal line for points."

For 60 minutes on this crisp fall Saturday in southeastern Cuba though, none of the arguments made in the ivory towers of American universities, the think tanks of Washington, or the halls of The Hague meant a thing. In between the white lines at Donald H. Rumsfeld Stadium at Gitmo, it was not the Geneva Accords but the law of the jungle that applied. One team fighting for its freedom. The other standing in the way.

The game was pure bloodsport, but it was surrounded by all the dazzling pageantry one would expect from an international spectacle of this magnitude. Burt Reynolds, the star of the original 1974 film *The Longest Yard*, presided over the ceremonial coin toss. *American Idol*'s season-three winner Fantasia Barrino belted out a stirring rendition of the National Anthem just before kickoff. A one-day moratorium on "walling" and waterboarding was called as the naval base at Guantánamo stood still.

The MPs, all of whose names have been redacted from this game summary by the United States Department of Defense, opened the game with a balanced drive, punctuated by a fourteen-yard touchdown pass from quarterback Lt. Col. ■■■■■■■ to his favorite target, tight end Capt. ■■■■■■■, that gave the MPs an early 7–0 lead. It was a sign of things to come in a dominant first half that saw the Guards take a commanding 21–0 lead into the halftime locker room.

As Toby Keith and the Jonas Brothers performed under a shower of fireworks on the field outside, FOX Sports cameras picked up part of the impassioned speech delivered by head coach Fazel Mazloom, the IED expert known as "Maz-Boom!," to his dejected Detainees.

"They say you're 'the worst of the worst.' And, you know what, maybe they're right. Maybe you are the worst. Maybe you don't deserve to be on the same field as the infidels over in that other locker room. Maybe we oughta just throw up the white flag right now, go back to our cells, and wait to die.

"I'll go tell the rear admiral over there that we're quitters. I'll tell him we've had enough. And someday, if we ever get out of here, you can tell your children you didn't have what it took to stand up to the Great Satan.

"But I'm not ready to do that, goddamn it! And when I

make the declaration to damn god, I mean their 'Christian' God, obviously! This is a Holy War, gentlemen! A clash of civilizations! This is your one chance to fight back! Let's get out there and beat these assholes so we can return to our native countries to resume terrorist activities, as opponents of the closing of this detention facility suspect we will! Can I get an 'Allahu Akbar!' up in this motherfucker?! Let me hear it! Allahu Akbar! Allahu Akbar! Let's go!!!"

Mazloom admitted later that he'd lifted portions of the speech from John Goodman's address to the Alpha Beta football players in *Revenge of the Nerds*. "How great is that movie?" Mazloom asked a reporter.

The Fightin' Detainees responded immediately to their coach's rousing speech, marching down the field on their captors to ring up a quick score right out of the locker room. They were flagged 15 yards for unsportsmanlike conduct when they pulled out prayer mats and prayed to Mecca in an orchestrated touchdown celebration. Mazloom said later, "I'll take that penalty. I love the enthusiasm. And so does Allah, by the way."

After dominating the Detainees in the first half, the Guards' offense went inexplicably dormant in the game's second 30 minutes. Quarterback Lt. Col. ■■■■■■■, a high school star from ■■■■■■■, Alabama, threw for 312 yards and 3 touchdowns, but he also gave up a pair of interceptions to Coach Mazloom's opportunistic defense. The second came with 5:41 left in the fourth quarter, when his receiver, First Sgt. ■■■■■■■, slipped on a crossing route, allowing ball-hawking Detainee safety and suspect in the kidnapping and torture of the families of Pakistani judges, Zafar Iqbal to step in front and return the pass for an easy touchdown, cutting the Guards' lead to 31–28. The Americans were stunned.

"■■■■■■■ and I got crossed up on that play. I probably shouldn't have thrown it," Lt. Col. ■■■■■■ said after the game. "That terrorist dude was in the right place at the right time. Hell, Saddam Hussein could have made that interception, and, as you know, he's dead."

After another stalled drive by the Guards, the Detainees would get the ball back one final time, trailing by that 31–28 margin with less than two minutes to play. Quarterback Raza was a picture of cool as he led his enemy combatants on the 86-yard march to freedom. Running the two-minute drill to perfection, Raza found Abdullah Al Yafii on consecutive first-down throws, the second bringing the Detainees to the Guards' three-yard line with 19 seconds to play.

What happened next will be the source of debate for generations in sports bars from Khartoum to Karbala, and Kabul to Casablanca. With the game hanging in the balance, Coach Mazloom called for a running play, despite the success of his passing game throughout the second half. The dastardly Raza turned and handed the ball to the militant Khan just as he'd done a thousand times before, but this time disaster struck. Khan took three steps and fumbled, the ball falling to the turf seemingly in slow motion. After a scrum, Army PFC ■■■■■■■ jumped from the pile with the ball raised high. The American sideline erupted in celebration. The game was over. The Detainees were put in leg shackles and returned to their cells.

"Yeah, I decided to run a little draw there. We still had a time-out if we didn't punch it in and our jihadist coaches upstairs saw something they liked in that defensive set," Coach Mazloom said after the game. "We just couldn't hold on to the football. In the end, this epic struggle of civilizations came down to fundamental football."

The quarterback Raza caused a stir in the locker room when he second-guessed the coach's decision to run the ball with the game on the line.

"I've been killing their defense all day like I'm the Messenger of Allah at the Battle of Badr, for Christ's sake, and all of a sudden we decide we're going to run the ball?" said a visibly frustrated Raza. "I don't get it, man. I don't get it. You have to ask who Coach Mazloom's really working for here. All I can say at this point is, death to the infidels. No more questions."

The Guards of the 525th Military Police Battalion at U.S. Naval Station Guantánamo Bay, Cuba, escaped with a narrow 31–28 victory, keeping the enemy combatants at the detention facility indefinitely and settling a question that had sparked emotional debate around the world. The President of the United States, Barack Obama, released a statement after the game.

"I am pleased with the effort of our men and women in uniform in today's game," Obama wrote in the statement. "With their uniquely American fight, determination, and persistence, these brave soldiers have, once and for all, taken the onus off me to make a decision on this vitally important issue. For that I am eternally grateful because, seriously, I had no clue what to do on this one. Whew.

"I'm also very pleased to have won my friendly bet with Osama bin Laden. I didn't want to have to part with all that Gino's Chicago-style deep-dish pizza. The month's supply of lamb kebabs is gonna taste a little extra sweet with this win. You've got the address, OBL."

The Al-Qaeda leader bin Laden was less gracious in an audiotape released after the game.

"That was some bullshit out there today!" said an emotional bin Laden. "How much did Obama pay those refs? Those two pass interference calls were both uncatchable balls! Next time just let me know the game is fixed beforehand so I don't waste four hours watching a lie. I had an entire 'Battle on the Bay' theme party in my cave for no reason. The place is a mess and I'm up to my ears in guacamole! And don't hold your breath on the kebabs, Obama. Boy, am I steamed."

Bin Laden's frustration with the officiating notwithstanding, the Detainees' surprisingly competitive performance on Saturday earned unlikely praise from their mortal enemies.

"I think the extremists, militants, and outright terrorists over there won a measure of respect with their effort today," said Guards head coach Navy Rear Admiral ■■■■■■■. "We expected them to roll over like the whiny little bitches they are, but they didn't. It's especially impressive when you consider we didn't allow them to wear football equipment. Just the turbans and flowing robes. Those guys put up a heck of a fight. Doesn't mean I'm not throwing 'em all into stress positions first thing tomorrow, but we'll certainly give 'em the night off."

The Detainees may have come up three yards short of freedom, but for just one bright afternoon on a breezy open field of fresh-cut green grass somewhere in the Caribbean, they were free to dream.

"This is a tough loss to swallow because we were so close. We allowed ourselves to think about life on the other side of that chain-link fence and it cost us," said the star receiver and bloodthirsty Yemeni radical Al Yafii. "No words will make it better. I mean, the words 'Death to America' always help, but this still stings. It'll just take time, which we've got plenty of now. On the bright side, how cool was it to meet Burt Reynolds? I'm a huge *Smokey and the Bandit* fan."

10

Oprah Is God

★

Since the very beginning of human history, scientists, philosophers, scholars, clerics, and just guys sitting around in bars have debated the existence of God. Now, a group of prominent American theologians has rocked the religious world with a new study that, they say, proves a higher power exists. So who, or what, is God and how can the authors of this potentially earth-shaking new research be so sure? They make their case in the latest edition of the quarterly academic journal *Harvard Theological Review.*

HARVARD THEOLOGICAL REVIEW

Harvard Divinity School
Cambridge, Massachusetts

"GOD IS OPRAH, OPRAH IS GOD"

Nearly a decade ago, a group of us were sitting around the faculty lounge at the Harvard Divinity School smoking clove cigarettes, drinking brandy, and talking about how frustratingly dumb most people are when a spirited argument broke out over the existence of God. We vowed that night, inside the walls of a smoke-filled room in Cambridge, that together we would author the definitive study on the subject. We also ended up taking some mescaline and playing a dangerous Tantric sex game with the folks in the Sanskrit and Indian Studies Department, but that is not germane to this report.

No matter how long it took us, we decided we would leave our mark as the mere mortals who answered humanity's oldest supernatural question: Is there a God? Today, after nine years of exhaustive research, we are proud and humbled to say that we have the answer.

God has been described over the course of human history as an intangible overseer of the universe. According to our findings, that characterization is only half true. God is omnipotent, but not intangible. In fact, God is a being of flesh and blood. God walks among us. God, you might be surprised to learn, has a talk show.

This study makes two important conclusions: 1) Yes, there is a God, and 2) God is Oprah Winfrey. Said another way, **Oprah is God.** *Can you believe it?! Just let that wash over you for a moment. Oprah Winfrey is God. Shocking at first, but then kind of starts to make sense, right?*

Oprah Winfrey has been a visible public figure for only the last 25 years, but our research shows She has been present for, and decisive in, everything that has ever happened in the history of the world. From the Big Bang to the Great War to every Miss Universe Pageant, Oprah's hand has been there pulling the strings and setting history on its course.

Trust me, we've heard all the old smug jokes about Oprah being "God," but this is not a joke. This is science. We have volumes of evidence that prove our case (the full report, as well as a variety of official Oprah Is God merchandise, can be found at our new flash website www.OprahIsGod.com, accessible for the low introductory price of $29.95/month).

So how did we get here? Our academic curiosity was piqued long ago by Oprah's peculiar power to influence human wants, needs, and purchasing habits. We wondered what kind of Supreme Being could cause grown women to hyperventilate at the simple mention of Her favorite top-load washer/dryer set? We struggled with the idea that a mere mortal could command an entire nation to buy and read books of Her choosing. And we doubted that someone who is not a deity would have the stones to put Herself on every cover of Her own magazine.

As we observed Oprah more closely, it became clear that She was leaving clues to Her true identity. She wanted to tell someone Her secret. It was our job as theologians to put the pieces of the puzzle together. Did that sound like something from The Da Vinci Code? *I hope so. I wanted it to.*

Nine long years of dissecting the ancient religious texts, of visiting the world's holiest sites, and of poring over back issues of O! *magazine confirmed our suspicion and proved our theory beyond a shadow of a doubt. The pieces fit. There was no longer any scientifically plausible way to deny that Oprah Winfrey is God.*

Oprah declined to be interviewed for our study, but when presented with the case made by the Harvard Divinity School, She confirmed in a formal letter that She is, in fact, God.

OPRAH WINFREY
HARPO PRODUCTIONS
Chicago, IL

Dean and Senior Faculty
Harvard Divinity School
Cambridge, MA 02138

Dear God Squad,

BUSTED! Yes, I am God. Guilty as charged. Congrats on cracking the code (finally). Look under your seat: you've won a new car! JK. You guys and Gayle are the only ones who

114

know. I haven't even told Stedman (I know, so bad, right?). I've got to say it feels pretty good to finally say it out loud. I am God! I am God! Wait, that sounds totally conceited. But you know what they say: it's not braggin' if it's true.

To be perfectly honest with you all, I'm a little ticked by the timing of your study because I was planning to do a big reveal on my show next month with Maya Angelou and Dr. Oz. I guess I'll just tell you now: we were going to pretend to tell Maya that Dr. Oz had a miracle treatment for her chronic arthritis and then instead: Surprise! I'm God! Can you imagine the look on Maya Angelou's face?! Would have been hilarious. With all due respect, the *Harvard Theological Review* wasn't quite the venue I had in mind to let the world know I am the Supreme Being. We were going to shut down Times Square for the announcement, have the Black Eyed Peas play, and give every person in the world a Bath & Body Works gift basket, but you got the scoop. I tip my cap. Talk about an "Aha!" moment for you guys, huh?

I don't have time to go through the whole story, but I'll try to answer some of your questions. Truthfully, I don't use words like "omnipotent," "divine," or "all-knowing." Those are labels others put on Me. If people want to capitalize pronouns when they talk about Me and fall to their knees when they address Me, that's up to them. It's not something I ever asked for. Between you and Me, I find it a little weird.

First things first: there's no such thing as polytheism, my friends. We can just put that to bed right now. I'm the only God. Sure, there are self-proclaimed "gods" out there, but it's like a philosophy PhD who wants to be called "doctor." If you can't take out my spleen, you ain't a doctor there, Kierkegaard. Same thing with gods. Everyone knows the real deal: there's Me and then there's everybody else.

Hey, can I clear up one thing? And please put this in your study. The Ten Commandments? Not Me. Moses was freelancing on that one. If I need a job done right, I don't outsource it. Don't get Me wrong, Mo blew up the spot on Mt. Sinai—the hand stonework on the tablets alone must have cost him a fortune—but I wasn't behind it. He went rogue. You see, I'm not one of these Gods who needs credit for everything. I mean, I control the tides of the planet's oceans and you don't see Me running around like My hair's on fire correcting people who claim the moon dictates tidal patterns.

I'm going to have to run into makeup in a minute here. I've got a woman backstage with a condition that turns her feet into pigs' hooves after sundown. She and her husband are coming on to talk about their ordeal. Now here's the hell of it: I'm God. I probably gave her that freaky disease. You start to lose track. And now I have to sit there and watch her cry about it. The guilt gets to you sometimes. Thank God I've got Kate Hudson for the second half of the show to cleanse the palate! Wait, did I just thank myself?! Anyway, let me dive into a few more of your questions before I split.

1. You asked about Jesus Christ. Let Me answer that with a line from Michael Jackson's hit single "Billie Jean": the kid is not my son. Not even related. The hero worship has spiraled wildly out of control over the last couple thousand years. I

haven't had the heart to tell everyone he was just a hippy dude from Nazareth who spent his days burning incense and playing with devil sticks.

2. On the whole Book of Genesis thing: as much as I'd like to say I have some David Copperfield magic wand I waved to bring about Heaven, Earth, water, and light, it's just not the way it went down. "Let there be light" makes a nice bumper sticker, but I never said it. The Earth was there when I got here. No idea where it came from, although I'm starting to come around on the whole Big Bang thing. Oh, and while we're on the subject, I guess now you know how David Copperfield's tricks work. A magician's big secret? ME! Although I have nothing to do with David Blaine. That is not magic. I don't get it. And, for the record, I feel horrible about the Siegfried and Roy thing.

3. World War II. I knew you'd ask about that. I've replayed this one in my head a million times. Hitler, Stalin, Mussolini, Pearl Harbor, two atomic bombs, and, what, 60 million dead? If I had it to do over again, I'd probably change some things, but I'm a "no regrets" kind of God. Let's just say I keep that one off the résumé and hope nobody asks. The only upside is that it makes everyone forget the First World War. That wasn't exactly my finest hour either.

Hey, how come no one ever talks about the Peloponnesian Wars? Everybody's so hung up on the twentieth-century bloodshed they forget Athens and Sparta had some pretty good scraps back in the ancient world. Everybody goes straight to Hitler. It's really frustrating. Look, I f★★ked up, okay? News flash: God is not perfect.

4. This is a strange one to focus on, but, yes, *Vegas Vacation* was My idea. Did I try to squeeze too much from the *Vacation* brand? Sure. It's tough to point fingers when you're the one who controls everything that happens in the universe, but I'll just say Chevy's heart was not in that picture.

5. Okay, one more here. The "Flutie Game"? Oh, boy. Okay, confession time: that was all Me. People call that Hail Mary touchdown pass by Doug Flutie to beat Miami back in '84 "a miracle." Well, only if you call it "a miracle" that I had 3,500 bucks riding on Boston College to win straight up. Yes, God works in "mysterious" ways. Especially when She needs a win to cover Her mounting losses at Arlington Park racetrack. Turns out harness racing is God's Achilles' heel.

There you have it. The word of God. Sorry I couldn't get to all your questions, but I refuse to apologize for every war, famine, and natural disaster in world history. Consider this a blanket apology for anything bad I've ever done. And for the record, I honestly never saw the O.J. thing coming. I mean, did you?

I don't want to seem unappreciative of your work, but you guys really harped on the negative in this study. If you'll permit a little PR spin from the Woman Upstairs, I would point you to flowers, rainbows, children's laughter, Monet, the Beatles,

Meryl Streep, Las Vegas, Captain Sully, *Maxim* magazine, sudoku, Cary Grant, the bald eagle, Xbox, cigarette boats, fireflies, and free online porn. Do you think that stuff just appeared out of thin air? No, that was Me. Oprah. God.

Print whatever you need here, guys. Just make Me look good, okay? You only get one shot to reveal to the world that you are God. And I am. Oprah is God!

All Best,

Oprah Winfrey (aka "God")
Follow me on Twitter @ www.twitter.com/God

p.s.—I had nothing to do with Crocs! We're looking into it.

TRUE STORY . . .

DROP THE LADY GILLETTE AND STEP AWAY FROM THE VEHICLE
Police: driver causes accident while shaving crotch

There's an old adage in the news business: if the story is weird as shit, it probably happened in Florida. That's why it was only a question of where in Florida a woman was arrested when she caused a two-car wreck while shaving her private parts behind the wheel. The 37-year-old woman was driving her 1995 Ford Thunderbird to meet her boyfriend in Key West and naturally she wanted to look her best. I'll be darned if her ex-husband wasn't making the trip with her and guiding the steering wheel while she trimmed her pubes. The teamwork that didn't quite work in their marriage failed them again as they slammed into a turning car during the shave.

Let's recap real quickly: a woman traveling with her ex-husband to visit her current boyfriend causes an accident while shaving her lady parts. Shall we continue or do you need a moment? Okay, on with the story.

Florida Highway Patrol trooper Gary Dunick was the first on the scene. He sees some strange things on the road through the Keys, but even by his high standard, the shaving-the-crotch-while-driving thing was impressive.

"About 10 years ago I stopped a guy in the exact same spot who had three or four syringes sticking out of his arm," said Trooper Dunick. "It was just surreal and I thought, 'Nothing will ever beat this.' Well, this takes it."

Just to add a little more flavor to the tale, the woman had been convicted of DUI the day before the driving-while-shaving accident. In fairness, the judge never said a word about not shaving behind the wheel. Her car was impounded and her license suspended for five years.

Let that be a lesson to all you youngsters: If you're thinking about having your ex-husband take the wheel while you shave your genitals on a trip to visit your boyfriend the day after you've been arrested for DUI, take a deep breath and think again.

11

Bernie Madoff: Welcome to Hell

★

SATAN'S CELEBRITY ROAST OF BERNIE MADOFF
With Your Roastmaster Pol Pot

A ll right, all right, everyone take your seats." The former genocidal Cambodian dictator Pol Pot taps the microphone at the podium. "Yeah, that means you, Mao: you might have outdone me by 40 million, but I'm runnin' this shit-show tonight. Have a seat, Chairman." Mao Zedong flips his buddy Pot a friendly middle finger before finding his way to a table.

Speaking over the din of the crowd, Pot begins the program. "Welcome to the John Wayne Gacy Room at the Hades Airport Radisson. First and foremost, where my Khmer Rouge dogs at?! It's Year Zero up in this bitch!" A group cheer comes from the back of the room. "Jesus, guys, nice seats back there. Who's your ticket broker, a Cambodian intellectual?" The line is met with muted laughter. A visibly frustrated Pot turns his sights on the audience. "Sorry, assholes, didn't mean to go over your heads there. I killed all the Cambodian intellectuals. They don't like me. Holy shit, am I gonna have to explain these all night? Genghis, I know you're a borderline caveman, but work with me here." The crowd laughs. Genghis Khan, not known for self-deprecation, does not laugh.

"But seriously, folks, I'm honored to be your roastmaster tonight as we welcome the newest celebrity member of this fiery little club we call Hell. It was a real thrill meeting Bernie Madoff back in the greenroom. I told him I wanted to diversify my portfolio and he told me, 'Great idea. Give half to me and half to my wife.'" This draws loud guffaws from the crowd as Madoff laughs and throws his hands in the air, resigned to the roasting he's about to receive.

"I don't know what it says about the depth of Bernie's evil, but when Satan met him he said, 'Welcome home, son.' Apparently a direct descendant of Lucifer." Madoff plays along, shrugging and nodding his head.

"The Devil wanted me to tell you he's sorry he couldn't be here tonight. He's reviewing Boy George's application for early admission down here. It's looking good for him." The lubed-up crowd loves it. "You hate to see one lousy incident where you chain a male hooker to your bedroom wall and beat him with a chain overshadow the years of music. Karma chameleon's a bitch though, ain't it?" More big laughs. Pot is on a roll.

"I want to introduce the all-star collection of sociopaths joining Bernie up here on the dais tonight. Please stand as you're recognized." Pot gestures from the podium down to the end of the long dais draped in fire-red bunting.

"Way down at the end there, the dean of this group, Mr. Pontius Pilate. Stand up, Ponty! Oh, that's right, you can't—you're two thousand goddamn years old!" The audience laughs and throws dinner rolls at Pilate, who sits in a wheelchair, not amused.

"Next to Ponty, a man whose numbers speak for themselves. Ladies and gentlemen, Uncle Joe Stalin!" Stalin, wearing full military regalia and clutching a half-empty bottle of Stolichnaya, staggers to his feet and waves, pointing at the table full of his fellow brutal dictators below and yelling, "Hey, 'Dolf, still think it was a good idea to invade us in '41? Have fun at the kids' table, shit-for-brains!" Mussolini doubles over in laughter as Adolf Hitler shoots him a glare.

Pot breaks up the fight. "All right, boys, settle down. Joe, leave some booze for the rest of us, huh?" Stalin takes a huge pull off the bottle, falls back into his seat, and puts his feet up on the dais. Hitler seethes in his chair. Madoff flashes a nervous smile and swallows hard. Hitler is quite intense in person.

Pot continues with the introductions. "Sitting right next to Bernie, a very special guest we invited just for the occasion, Mr. Charles Ponzi. Chuck, say hello to everyone." Ponzi, unassuming and dressed in a vintage 1920s three-piece suit, stands and doffs his bowler. He is not a regular on the Hades A-list social circuit and receives only lukewarm applause.

"That's the original right there, folks. Let's give Chuck Ponzi a nice welcome. Come on!" Pot prods the crowd. "Jesus Christ, Mother Teresa, if I told you he had leprosy would you get off your sweet little ass and clap for the guy? " Mother Teresa cracks a forced smile, unable to mask the bitterness she still harbors about the epic bureaucratic snafu shortly after her death that led to her being sentenced to an eternity in the fires of Hell. In a statement released after the mix-up, God called the incident "unfortunate," saying, "Mistakes were made." Heads rolled in Heaven after that one.

Pot senses Mother Teresa doesn't appreciate the ribbing. "I'm just fuckin' with ya, Terry. Don't get your habit in a bunch down there." The crowd roars with laughter. Mother Teresa begins to weep. "Oh, Christ. Somebody get her a napkin." Pot is annoyed.

"All right, back to the introductions. To my left, one of the greatest running backs in NFL history, and a world-famous cold-blooded murderer, Mr. Orenthal James Simpson." A crowd favorite, O.J. draws whoops and hollers.

"Remember, the Juice will be signing Buffalo Bills mini-helmets and copies of his book *If I Did It* immediately after our program tonight. Good to see you, Juice.

"Seated next to O.J., that pain in the ass Lee Harvey Oswald."

Oswald stands and shouts, "It was him!," pointing to Sam Giancana, who is seated at a table playing dominos with Al Capone and John Gotti. Giancana looks up momentarily before turning back to his game.

The crowd boos Oswald, lobbing a barrage of dinner rolls in his direction.

Pot leans into the microphone. "You are such a little bitch, Oswald. I don't know why we invite you to these things. Have a seat, lone gunman."

"It was the Cubans!" Oswald shouts feebly, before sitting down in a hail of stale bread.

Pot, who has stated publicly his belief that Oswald gives communists a bad name, ups the ante. "Is Jack Ruby in the house? We need to shut that little weasel up."

The crowd laughs at Pot's zinger. Oswald shoots back sternly, "Too far, dude. Not funny. There's a line, man."

Pot ignores Oswald and continues.

"And seated all the way down at the end there, the Reverend Jim Jones. He's the shithead who thought he heard God tell him to lead a bunch of mouth-breathers and their helpless kids down to Guyana for a little mass suicide Kool-Aid party."

Reverend Jones, dressed in a late seventies-era white suit, smiles, stands up halfway out of his chair, and raises his glass to the crowd. There is no applause. Pot looks disgusted. Jones sits down quickly.

"Look, I'm not riding any high horses up here, but at least I was upfront about my intentions: to completely wipe out the culture, history, and people of Cambodia and start that shit from scratch. I was a straight shooter.

"Those poor bastards at Jonestown thought they were going down to some kind of a summer camp to play tetherball and tell ghost stories. Next thing they know, some sweaty bisexual preacher is handing out shots of cyanide-flavored fruit juice. Not cool, Reverend."

Jones, feeling the judgmental glare of the group, looks down at his plate and ponders the concept of a moral lecture from Pol Pot.

"Word to the wise: if Reverend Jones offers to buy you a drink tonight, take a pass, if you know what I mean."

The crowd likes that one. The tension of the moment is broken. Even Jones allows himself a grin before power-chugging his drink and collapsing to the floor.

With the introductions complete, Pol Pot proceeds with the evening's program. "I see I'm not going to have the attention of you lushes for long, so just a couple of housekeeping items before we let this fuckin' thief over here say a few words." Madoff chuckles and shakes his head.

"First, where's Jeffrey Dahmer?" Pot shields his eyes from the lights and scans the crowd. "Is Dahmer here?" The serial killer looks up from his plate and raises his hand. "Oh, there you are. Yeah, Jeff, the chef wanted me to make sure you know there will be an hors d'oeuvres course, so you can stop nibbling on the Menendez brothers' ears." The crowd roars with laughter. Dahmer stares straight ahead, emotionless, his eyes hidden behind orange-tinted sunglasses. "That goes for you too, Idi

Amin. Try not to eat any humans tonight. You cocksuckers
ruined Ted Bundy's birthday party last year."

"Let's see, what else? Oh, Saddam. Saddam Hussein, are you
in the room?" Saddam stands and fires a rifle into the air. "There
he is! Yeah, Saddam, we just got a telegram from George W.
Bush." The crowd boos the mention of Bush's name. Pot talks
over the interruption. "Really? Again, guys, I'm pretty sure we
don't get to pass judgment down here. I'm just sayin'. I mean,
'Dolf, seriously. I don't want to tell you your business, but I'd just
lay low if I were you." Hitler grimaces and goose-steps out of the
banquet room.

Pot rolls his eyes. "What a petulant little man. Anyway,
Saddam, Bush just wants you to know he's sorry about every-
thing. Says he meant to invade and later execute the leader of
Iran, not Iraq. Bush writes simply, 'Dear Saddam. My bad.
The word "Iraq" looks like "Iran" when they're making you
sign the war thing and you've got one eye on the Home Run
Derby—Jason Giambi was really jerking those things out of the
yard that night. So I was one letter off. Sue me. Shit happens.
No hard feelings. Hope we're cool. XOXO, Dubya.' "

Saddam throws his head back, lets out a big laugh, and fires
three quick rounds into the ceiling. Pot jumps in, "Whoa, whoa,
this isn't one of your goddamn gilded castles in Ramadi! We're
not gonna get our security deposit back here." Saddam puts his
hands up as if to say "Sorry" and sits down.

"If we've all got our firearms holstered, for Christ's sake, I'd
like to formally introduce our honoree. You know, I've known
Bernie Madoff for only an hour and somehow I've already lost

my life savings. Hold on to your wallets around this blood-sucking scam artist." Madoff jokingly makes a move toward Pol Pot's wallet.

"I don't want to re-litigate history here, but I dare anyone in this room to look at the greedy capitalist pig sitting over there and tell me I was wrong about killing everyone and starting over with an agrarian society." The crowd really enjoys where Pot is going. "Actually, Bernie, I had you in mind when I came up with the idea." Pot gestures to the Khmer Rouge table in the back of the room. "In fact, get him, boys!" The crowd roars. Bernie gets halfway out of his chair as if to run for the exit.

"I'm just fuckin' with you, Bernie. Water under the bridge, my man. This isn't about me. This is your night." As the laughs die down, Pot's expression changes.

"Just to be serious for a moment, if I could. We honor a man tonight who ran a $65 billion scheme that erased lifetimes' worth of work and tore apart families. He fleeced hospitals, charities, and even golfing buddies to line his own pockets. His evil knows no bounds. I can tell you now, Bernie, that you were voted into this elite club of the Worst Human Beings to Ever Walk the Earth unanimously and without objection." Madoff nods in appreciation.

"With that, I will just say, Mr. Bernard L. Madoff, welcome to Hell." Madoff receives a standing ovation as he walks to the podium. Pot hands Madoff an engraved Waterford crystal bowl and shakes his hand as the pair poses for a photographer who has rushed to the front of the podium. When the applause stops, Madoff addresses the microphone.

"Thank you, Pol. Thank you all very much. Please, please be seated." Madoff scans the crowd and stops on one member of the audience. "Is that Harry Truman? Really? Kind of surprised to see you here." The former United States president throws up his hands in frustration as if to say, "You're tellin' me."

"I was sorry to see Hitler leave earlier. I've got a bone to pick with that guy on behalf of some of my friends back on the Upper East Side." The crowd laughs at Madoff's good-natured icebreaker.

"Look, I'll be brief here. When I look out at the faces I see in this room tonight, it's kind of hard for me to believe I'm worthy of your company. You are truly the worst people in the history of human civilization. Except for you, Mother Teresa. I mean, how does that happen?" Mother Teresa begins to weep again.

"I should first give a nod to Charles Ponzi for laying the blueprint. You are the Dr. J to my Michael Jordan. Without you, there is no me. Thank you, Chuck." Ponzi tips his bowler again.

"I guess in my heart I always knew I'd end up here. When I was taking all that money from little old ladies to buy rare African art for my place in Montauk or ripping off children's charities to put an infinity pool and one of those big, industrial-size outdoor grills in the place in Palm Beach, I knew it was wrong, but evil is addictive—am I right, Joseph Stalin?"

Madoff looks down the dais to Stalin, who is passed out face-first in a pool of his own vomit. Mussolini is drawing a penis on his face with a black Sharpie. Madoff is losing the room.

"Anyway, I'm honored to be here in Hell. It's a lot better than making license plates in a federal prison for 12 cents a day. That was just demeaning for a man of my means." Madoff gets a laugh from the crowd.

"And my sincere thanks to Pol Pot for hosting tonight's event. You're overshadowed in the history books by other twentieth-century dictators, but let it not be forgotten that you are one of the biggest assholes in the history of the planet—and one hell of a roastmaster.

"One last thing: I know it sounds crazy, but please do look me up when considering your financial future. Eternity is a long time: are you ready? Thank you all for your kind welcome to Hell." Pot comes to the podium and gives Madoff a long hug as the crowd applauds.

As the guests begin to disperse, Pot rushes to the microphone with one last announcement. "Hang on, gang. Before you leave, we want to let everyone know that Pablo Escobar has been kind enough to host the after-party at his compound tonight. One important note: if you decline his invitation, members of your family will be executed in public and fed to exotic crocodiles for Pablo's personal entertainment. See you all there."

12

Go-karts and Waterslides: The George W. Bush Presidential Library

★

George Walker Bush, the forty-third president of the United States, has been involved intimately in the planning of his presidential library and museum on the campus of Southern Methodist University in Dallas. President Bush has been especially generous with his time since he was relieved, by a unanimous coaches' vote, of his duties as commissioner of the Highland Park Little League Association. One team mother called Bush's tenure as commissioner "a complete f**king mess." Mr. Bush has called his removal as commissioner "unconstitutional" and the public criticism of his performance "probably unconstitutional." The president's tumultuous three months in that position will not be included in the museum, library, or public policy institute that bears his name.

President Bush has insisted, in the spirit of a full accounting of his legacy (except for the Little League thing), that the very first planning and development memorandum he sent to the executive committee of the George W. Bush Presidential Center become part of the historical record preserved there. He didn't have to make this public, mind you. We tried to protect him, but he's proud of the document. He calls it his "Jerry Maguire moment." Wants it framed and hung inside the center's main entrance next to the display of "The President's Favorite Sluggers," a collection of baseball players' posters that includes those of Frank Thomas, Rafael Palmeiro, and Boog Powell.

In fact, Mr. Bush wants visitors to be able to sift through a compilation of all his presidential e-mails in what he envisions as "one of those cool hologram information things Tom Cruise used to solve crimes in *Minority Report*." President Bush likes Tom Cruise movies . . . a lot. Especially *Days of Thunder* and *Cocktail*.

Bear in mind, we've quietly ignored most of the ideas you're about to read. He absolutely will not budge, however, on the go-kart track.

To: staff@gwbushlibrary.gov
From: Prez43@yahoo.com
Re: George W. Bush Presidential Center

What's shakin' y'all! I don't mean to brag right out of the gate, but I just beat my all-time high score on Centipede. I took a Polaroid of the screen and sent it in to Atari. I think they send you a plaque or an iron-on patch or something. I'll put it down there in the basement with all the weird crap those African presidents give you when you visit (thanks for the sawed-off elephant tusk, Prime Minister Mugatu. Anyone have any idea what I'm supposed to do with this thing?). Anyway, I guess you could say I made a little presidential history downstairs in the A/V room today.

Little known fact (and we should throw this in the library some-where): in 1997, Jeb and I competed in "The Bush Olympics" up at Kennebunkport to decide who'd get to run for president. He won sport fishing and movie trivia. I won hold-your-breath-underwater, home run derby, and Centipede. Guess what? I'm president. I don't even know what Jeb does these days (I want to say lawyer? Banker? Tailor? One of those).

Anyway, I guess we've gotta do this library/museum thing. Honestly, I'd just as soon erase those eight years from the record books like they were Barry Bonds's career stats and go back to the jai alai fronton for the rest of the afternoon. I mean, do people really want to visit a place to *relive* that nightmare? I seriously doubt it. Jesus Christ, it was horrible the first time. Trust me. I was there. Having said all that, I want you to know I really appreciate all the work you've been doing to make this president center happen. It's not your fault that it's a terrible, terrible idea. I can tell you one thing: we're gonna do it our way.

This is kind of like a manifesto (à la *Jerry Maguire*—Show me the money!). I'll fire off a few thoughts for you to chew on, but my big headline (and I'll preach this until I'm blue in the face) is DO NOT MAKE THIS THING ALL LIBRARY-ISH!! I'll say it again because I don't want there to be any confusion: DON'T MAKE MY PRESIDEN-TIAL LIBRARY ALL LIBRARY-ISH!! In fact, let's not call it a library at all. People hate libraries. Reminds them of school and late fees. Why would we build something people hate? Instead we're gonna call it an Entertainment SuperPlex. Comprenday? ("Understand" in Spanish.)

Our SuperPlex won't be all stuffy and quiet and full of boring books about presidents nobody's ever heard of (i.e., Frank Pierce, Jimmy K. Polk, Millard Fillmore [Caution! Nerd name!], etc.). I used to go to my dad's museum over in College Station to hear speeches by Hank Kissinger and Rummy and I'd look around while they were rambling on and think to myself, "This place is screaming for a batting cage." So we WILL have batting cages at my Entertainment SuperPlex. That's an executive order! (I just like saying that now—those dicks never listened when I used to say it in the Oval Office.) Sounds important and forceful, like Harrison Ford in that movie *Air Force One*—"Get off my plane!" Great flick.

So here's the mission: make this a place where people would actually WANT to go. Our competition isn't another snoozer library full of geeks and presidential groupie freaks who like sniffing the ink on old Oval Office memos. Our competition is Six Flags Over Texas, which is full of awesome party people who wear tank tops, jean shorts, and Tevas. Six Flags has the Shock Wave roller coaster. What do we have? Policy papers on Medicare and a stapler off John

Ashcroft's desk? *Zzzzzzzzzzz* . . . sorry, I fell asleep for a second there. That was not for effect. I literally fell asleep in the middle of writing a sentence.

You think a bunch of eighth graders on a field trip want to look at some bullshit about the Sarbanes-Oxley Act? Hell no! They want water-slides! So let's give 'em waterslides! Two waterslides, in fact: one open-topped with tons of twists and a huge drop at the end and then one of those scary covered ones where you can't see anything 'til you get right to the end. Jesus, I just pissed my pants thinkin' about it! And a wave pool. And an IMAX theater with a snack counter that sells Twizzlers. This SuperPlex is gonna be so much cooler than my dad's presidential dork-out center.

I'll be interested to hear your thoughts on the George W. Bush Kick-ass SuperPlex (remember, NO nerd ideas), but let's get these ones in the pipeline ASAP while they're on the top of my head. I'll forget 'em while I'm bonefishing with Sammy Hagar down in Cabo for the rest of the month. Write these babies down:

1. America vs. Terrorists laser tag played in a big, dark warehouse full of swarthy-lookin' actors to play the Taliban dudes. Reminds people we kept them safe for 7 years.

2. Interactive John Yoo Torture Memo Experience. (Make this fun and kid-friendly—lighten up a touchy issue. Waterboarding dunk tank? Let's think.)

3. "Bush Munchers" Food Court (with "Heck-of-a-Job Brownies!" bakery and definitely a Quiznos).

4. "Rock and Rove" Karaoke Thursday nights. Ladies drink free, 9 p.m.–?????

5. Wrestling matches with those hilarious giant sumo fat suits. Those crack me up!

6. Dick Cheney/Condi Rice salt-and-pepper shakers at the gift shop. (See, he's white and she's black. Salt and pepper. How great is that?!) Also "the Decider" trucker caps.

7. Nolan Ryan autograph booth.

8. "No Child Left Behind" kiddie coaster.

9. Go-karts, go-karts, go-karts! (Must have mini-golf and chocolate chip cookie dough ice cream.)

10. The Harriet Miers 24-hour Steakhouse and Titty Bar.

Important note: Let's put the Iraq and Katrina stuff on the top floor with a clever sign that says MISSION NOT YET ACCOMPLISHED! WE'RE REMODELING . . . blocking the stairs so no one goes up there. That stuff is a bummer and could ruin an otherwise awesome day of go-karts, waterslides, and karaoke at the George W. Bush Presidential Entertainment SuperPlex.

As you all know, nothing is more important to a president than his legacy. How will history remember the guy? Well, if we go with what we've got now, I'm screwed in that department. The San Francisco hippies at *Rolling Stone* said I might be the worst president ever. Of course they were all high on mushrooms and having gay sex with each other when they said that, but that's what I'm up against out there. Gay hippy druggie college professors are the ones who write the history books. The rest of us have real jobs.

It's our job right now to get the focus off the WMDs of yesterday and onto the funnel cakes and free pony rides of tomorrow. Let's rewrite history together, my friends. This is our time.

Peace and love,

W.

TRUE STORY . . .

DUDE, WHERE'S MY WEED?
Man calls 911 to report stolen marijuana

We could argue all day about whether or not marijuana is physically harmful or whether or not it should be legal, but that's a conversation for another day. Okay, let's argue for just a second: it's not harmful and it should be legal. Anyway, whatever your position on the decriminalization of pot, one thing I think we can all agree on is that weed makes you dumb as hell.

Just ask the 21-year-old Salem, Oregon, man who called 911 to report to police that his marijuana had been stolen. Police are of course the state and municipal officials charged with enforcing the laws of the land—so not the first people to turn to when your drugs go missing. According to the cops, the man called the emergency number furious because someone had broken into his truck outside the Free Loader Tavern in Salem and stolen his jacket, $400 in cash, and, yes, just shy of an ounce of marijuana.

Now maybe you write that off as a drunken fluke if it happens once, but the guy called 911 an hour later to complain that police had not yet responded to his first report of the stolen weed. For my money, the best line of the local news report on the incident was as follows: "The dispatcher had trouble understanding [the man], who stopped several times to throw up." Yes, he was driving around looking for the people who stole his weed, stopping occasionally to barf by the side of the road.

Police eventually found the man and arrested him on charges of driving while intoxicated. They could not file drug charges because, as you'll remember from the man's repeated 911 calls, there was no marijuana. Someone had stolen it.

13

Parenting Magazine: Five Questions with Kate Gosselin

★

*P*arenting magazine continues its celebration of Celebrity Moms Month with our latest installment of "Five Questions for _____." Today, reality TV star, author, and mother of eight Kate Gosselin dishes about that hair, that ex-husband, and, oh yeah, all those kids. *Parenting* caught up with the busy mom at the star-studded after-party for the new season of *The Biggest Loser*.

PARENTING: So, how are the kids?

KATE GOSSELIN: I think they're doing really well, thanks. We just had a sixth birthday party for the sextuplets at the Viper Room in West Hollywood. It was sponsored by Cîroc vodka and Axe Body Spray.

A couple of the girls from *The Real Housewives of Atlanta* stopped by. Dina Lohan was there. It was so awesome. The kids wanted to have one of those super-lame cupcake parties at school with their friends, but thank God my friend Kristin Cavallari from *The Hills* stepped up to throw me the party.

Those six little birthday angels flew out on Joe Francis's jet and spent most of the night napping in the VIP room with Verne Troyer. They must have been wiped out from having so much fun! Also, it was four a.m. and they're six years old. Verne drove them home. He's such a sweetie.

PARENTING: Now that you've had some time to reflect on the impact *Jon & Kate Plus Eight* had on your family, if you could go back in time, would you invite the TV cameras into your life again?

KG: Uh, let me think: Yes! If it weren't for that show, I'd still be a nurse at some s**tbox hospital in Pennsylvania, I'd still be married to Jonny Jerkoff, and I certainly wouldn't be on a first-name basis with any of the Real Housewives. I've noticed that Pennsylvania nurses married to d-bags with no job don't make it on Barbara Walters's list of "Most Fascinating People" all that often. The minute I unloaded Daddy Dead Weight, I made the "Most Fascinating" list. No one can ever take that away from me. My only regret is that the cameras didn't come a few years sooner. I would have dumped Ed Hardy and gone after Mario Lopez a long time ago.

PARENTING: But, as you know, our focus is on parenting and the unique challenges every parent faces. Don't you think it's difficult to give your children a normal upbringing when their lives are broadcast on national television?

KG: The children cried when I sat them down last year and told them the show was canceled, okay? They absolutely loved being on TV. I'll never forgive Jon for taking that piece of their childhood away from them. I mean, the producers and cameramen were like part of the family. Especially Lorenzo, the tan, muscular sound guy—most of the kids called him Daddy because he was so much cooler than their real dad. Also, because Lorenzo often slept in my bed when Jon was passed out down on the couch watching *SportsCenter.* It was so nice finally to share a pillow with a real man. Lorenzo smelled like the leather of a freshly oiled horse saddle.

So, no, the kids probably haven't had a normal upbringing, but "normal" doesn't pay the bills. Know what I mean? Just last week, the twins did an appearance at the grand opening of a batting cage back home. Boom! That's three grand right there! Weekend before that, a bunch of the sextuplets dressed up like the Little Rascals for a bachelor party in Las Vegas—first class travel, a suite at Bally's, totally comped at the tables, the works. God, I wish I could have been there to see that. Hilarious!

PARENTING: Your 6-year-olds went to a bachelor party in Las Vegas? And you weren't there? Wow. Perhaps we should change the subject. Why do you think people are so fascinated by your hair?

KG: It's so funny, I was having lunch at the Cheesecake Factory the other day with JWoWW from *Jersey Shore* and she was like, "Girlfriend, your hair is, like, famous!" It was funny because I had never thought of hair as being famous, but it's totally true. So I'm like, "Hello! Your hair is way more famous than my hair!" We seriously argued for like 10 minutes about it. Then we crushed some Peanut Butter Cup Fudge cheesecake. Have you ever had that? Uh! So good!

But I'm flattered that people think my hair is cool. Like most busy moms, I don't have much time to think about the way I look. I mean, I wake up early with the kids, send them to the craft service table for breakfast, and then whatever my round-the-clock hair and makeup team does with my hair in the trailer is the way it looks all day. Who has time?! So if I'm a style icon or whatever—and *In Touch Weekly* did say so in its recent "Hottest Reality Stars" issue—it's purely by accident. I just think of myself as a regular old mom.

PARENTING: Last question: can you name all eight of your children?

KG: Excuse me? Of course I can. That's ridiculous. [*laughter*] You seriously expect me to do that for you?

PARENTING: Yes, your kids' names. Many of our readers are expectant parents looking for the perfect name for their new baby. So what are your children's names? All of them.

KG: I'm completely offended by your question, but I know what happens if I don't answer—front-page headline of *OK!* next week says "Kate Doesn't Know Her Own Kids' Names!" I've played this game before. So here you go. There are the twins, Cara and Mady. Then there's the big group of six that I always mess up: There's Alexis,

Hannah, uh, then you've got, uh, oh, s**t—it's something weird. I wanna say Aaron, but that's not it. [*Publicist leans into Gosselin's ear.*] Aaden! I knew it was an "A." Then you have, uh, oh Christ, I don't know—Donny and Marie, and, uh, Tito and LaToya— Hey! Look over there! [*Gosselin points behind reporter. Reporter turns around. Gosselin runs out of the room.*]

Editor's Note: Next week's "Five Questions for _____," originally scheduled to be with Whitney Houston, has been changed. We could not find her. Instead, Dog the Bounty Hunter talks about balancing kids with the pursuit of fugitives across state lines.

14

The Kim Jong-il
Celebrity Golf Tournament

★

Y ou are looking at breathtaking aerial pictures of the Democratic People's Golf and Racquet Club on another beautiful afternoon in Pyongyang, North Korea, home of the 7th Annual Kim Jong-il Celebrity Golf Challenge, right here on CBS . . ."

The slow, drippy piano music fades out and the picture dissolves from the overhead shot of the course to the announcers' booth. Two Western-looking men wearing blue blazers with the CBS Sports logo stitched onto the pocket sit framed by a pair of Asian men in matching gray suits who are standing with their hands clasped perfectly and staring ahead blankly.

"Hello, friends, I'm Jim Nantz, joined in the booth by my partner, the three-time Masters champion Nick Faldo . . . and by our two government minders, who have been nothing but gracious and patriotic since our arrival here in North Korea. Some say this country is an outpost of tyranny run by a nutty little guy who wears women's pantsuits from Chico's. I say . . ." Nantz looks down at his notes, clears his throat, and reads, "Those people are Western imperialists who, mark the words of the Dear Leader Kim Jong-il, will suffer grave consequences if they light the fuse of war on the Korean peninsula."

Nantz exhales and puts the note card to the side. The men in gray suits nod subtly in approval.

"Our aerial coverage is provided as always by a surveillance blimp from the good people at the National Defense Commission of North Korea, who remind you that 'Someone is always watching.'"

"With that, Nick Faldo, we begin another year in what really has become the premiere celebrity golf tournament in the world."

"There's no question about it, Jimmy. The players and the celebrities love to come here to Pyongyang every year—mostly, let's just be honest, because of the outrageous purse for the field. Ten million dollars, a Russian MiG-21 fighter jet, and a newborn baby just for showing up is a little better than what they offer at the John Deere Classic!" Nantz chuckles nervously. Faldo glances over his shoulder at the hovering government agent and then looks down at a note card of his own.

"But they also enjoy the tournament because this is a lovely, peaceful country—nothing like it is portrayed in the West. Just from my short time here I can tell you that the international reports of rampant poverty, violent suppression of opposition, and leadership by a man who died four years ago and now runs the country *Weekend at Bernie's*–style are completely false and irresponsible." Faldo takes a deep breath. "Those who continue to perpetuate such falsehoods should prepare to face a firestorm of nuclear retaliation." Faldo looks up from the card at Nantz.

"Indeed, Nick. Let's take a look at some of the fascinating groups that'll be out there on this immaculate course today.

"We begin with our host, the Dear Leader Kim Jong-il.* He was first off the tee this morning, playing in his handpicked group with the legendary former coach of the Chicago Bears, Mike Ditka, and funnyman Ray Romano. Looks like they're having some fun out there already. Let's send it down to our colleague David Feherty with that group just stepping off the tenth green. David?"

"Thanks, Jimmy. I have the good fortune to be here with the Dear Leader himself—" Kim Jong-il jumps in. "David, please, call me Chairman. Or Supreme Commander. My father was the Dear Leader! You're makin' me feel old over here."

Feherty proceeds, "All right, Mr. Supreme Commander, another year, another really first-rate event."

"Well, first of all, none of this is possible without our sponsors. Let's be real clear about that. Big shout-out to the gang at Outback Steakhouse. They really stepped up again this year. Uh, State Farm, Bob Sanders and his team over there—can't say enough about the commitment they've made to this event. And I don't want to congratulate myself too much, but it certainly doesn't hurt the ol' bottom line when you peddle outrageous amounts of nuclear material on the international black market as I did this year. What recession, right?"

* Played by one of those pastel little bingo dolls shaped like naked Neanderthal infants with day-glo Don King hair.

Feherty replies, "Whatever you say, Supreme Commander. Now, tell us about this group you've assembled today. Why'd you pick Ray Romano?"

"Because Ted Danson wasn't available!" Kim Jong-il cracks himself up and punches Romano in the arm. Romano laughs politely because if he doesn't he'll be executed.

"No, look, I'm a big fan of Ray's. I actually tried to kidnap him and the cast of *Everybody Loves Raymond* a few years ago to make them perform an entire season of the show in one of my bunkers, but the plot was foiled by those dicks at the CIA. An abduction is the biggest compliment I can pay an artist."

Romano nods. "True story."

Feherty moves on. "Wow, you *are* a big fan. And the third member of this group, Mike Ditka."

"Yes, Iron Mike. Get over here, Mike, ya big lug." Kim Jong-il throws his arm around Ditka, who laughs and picks Kim Jong-il off the ground in a giant bear hug. Ditka is wearing a Panama Jack straw hat and an ironic T-shirt with a picture of Kim Jong-il that reads, YOU BE IL-IN'!

"This guy is the best," says the Dear Leader. "I modeled my leadership style after Ditka when he was with those great Bears teams of the eighties—disciplined, tough, and afraid of no one. Only difference, I guess, is that Ditka didn't starve millions of his own people." Kim Jong-il lets out a big laugh. "Kidding, kidding. Relax, everybody. It's a joke."

Kim Jong-il turns to Ditka. "Although maybe you should have starved the Fridge—guy could have used a little less time at the dessert cart. Jesus." Ditka laughs and puts Kim Jong-il into a playful headlock. Ditka is quickly tackled to the ground and thrown into an unmarked car.

Feherty tries to move on. "All right, well, hit 'em straight on the back nine and have fun out there, Supreme Commander."

Kim Jong-il pulls out a completed scorecard and waves it in Feherty's face. "Hit 'em straight? Dudn't matter how I hit 'em, you wacky Irish bastard. Here's my completed scorecard for today's round. Let's see . . ." Kim Jong-il holds the card away from himself and looks down his glasses deliberately.

"Whoa, looky there! Six holes in one! Looks like another good day for the Big Man, David! I *always* hit 'em straight, dumb-ass! You must be new here. We'll see you at the bar—that's one place I know an Irishman like you can find." Kim Jong-il slaps Feherty on the back and turns for the next tee. "Let's go, boys. We've got Putin and George Lopez breathin' down our necks in that group behind us!"

Kim Jong-il turns and shouts to Vladimir Putin, *Played by Daniel Craig* who is putting on the tenth green, "Hey, Vlad! Double or nothing on those warheads says you blow that putt!"

Putin steps away from his putt and turns over his shoulder to Kim Jong-il. "Maybe if you hadn't mowed all these greens in the exact image of your own face, I wouldn't have to putt around your giant forehead, Mr. Supreme Egomaniac! Oh, and I didn't know they made platform golf spikes!"

Kim Jong-il bursts into a giant laugh. Putin smiles and waves his hands dismissively at the Dear Leader. George Lopez and the third member of their group, former NFL quarterback Vinny Testaverde, look at each other and decide it's a good idea to laugh.

Feherty kicks it back up to the booth. "Well, Jimmy, our host putting on another good show today."

"And what a showman he is, David Feherty. Thank you." Nantz turns back to his partner.

"Nick Faldo, let's go out to the 4th tee, where we find the compelling group of Iranian president Mahmoud Ahmadinejad, Hall of Fame catcher Johnny Bench, and our good friend Maury Povich. This group, Nick, really playing some good golf this week."

"Yeah, Jimmy, Maury is playing well, as he always does. The big surprise here, frankly, is Ahmadinejad. He is surprisingly long off the tee for a man his size. He looks great tee-to-green. He's missed some putts that he'd probably like to have back, but really quite impressive with the long irons."

Nantz nods, adding, "And despite the warm conditions, the Iranian president playing in that zip-up windbreaker he has made so famous. The jacket this week though adorned with the logos for Baked! Lays and General Electric—some of us surprised to see American sponsors attracted to the man who has wished publicly for the annihilation of the United States of America.

"Let's go down to another member of our broadcast team today, Gary McCord. He's with President Ahmadinejad, who just bombed one off the tee. Sounds like that one cleared the DMZ, Gary."

"Thanks, Jimmy. Great geopolitical reference. I'm here with the Iranian president, whose name I won't even attempt to pronounce. Mr. President, pretty handy with a three-wood in your hand there, sir."

Ahmadinejad leans into the microphone. "Thanks, Gary. I don't get to play as much as I'd like to, but when K-Jong calls, I ask where he wants me and when. He's like a brother. We stay in touch mostly over our shared Axis of Evil Facebook page."

McCord nods like all good sideline reporters do when they're listening to complete nonsense.

"Plus, what a thrill to meet the great Johnny Bench, right? What kid didn't want to be Johnny Bench growing up? I had posters of him, the Ayatollah, and Dominique Wilkins on the wall over my bed. Don't tell the Supreme Council, but the Johnny Bench poster was the biggest." Ahmadinejad winks at the camera and chuckles.

"I told Johnny back in the clubhouse over a chicken salad sandwich and an Arnold Palmer that I'd give him a couple days warning before I wipe the United States off the map so he can go to Toronto for the weekend. Him and Carson Daly. Those are literally the only two people I'm telling." Ahmadinejad laughs at his own joke. "Just teasing, guys. No, I'm not."

McCord struggles with a reply to the statement. "Uh, I think he means it, guys. Jimmy, let's go back up to you." Ahmadinejad waves to the camera and mouths, "Hi, Mom! Death to America!" as they cut back to Nantz and Faldo in the booth.

"Thank you, Gary. Sounds to me like he definitely intends to destroy America. Nick, you're British so you absolutely could not care less. Let's get back to the golf. Quite a collection of talent out on the course today—walk us through some of the really interesting groups playing together."

"Just delicious combinations here, Jimmy. We know that Kim Jong-il has already signed a card showing he shot a 48 today even though he still has 8 holes to play, so these other players are really going for second place." Faldo's government minder takes a step toward him.

"I'll be watching the threesome of Hugo Chávez, Samuel L. Jackson, and rocker Alice Cooper very closely. Some really good golfers in that group. Alice Cooper takes a backseat to no one on the golf course, as you know. In fact, celebrity golf is actually all a new generation knows of him. And Sam Jackson, of course, has turned into one of the best celebrity players out there. He wears Kangol caps sideways when he plays. That kind of an urban look makes many people around the course quite nervous. I like it, but that doesn't mean I don't hold my wallet a little tighter when he's around."

Nantz nods in agreement as Faldo continues.

"Now Chávez had requested Danny Glover in his group, of course, but Glover is currently in postproduction on a porn version of *Lethal Weapon* called, ironically, *Lethal Weapon*. Harry Belafonte originally was scheduled to be in the Chávez group as well, but sadly, he got lost looking for his shoes. He was last seen signing an autograph for a mannequin at a Los Angeles–area men's shop."

Nantz jumps in. "And, Nick, let's go down to the seventh, where I'm told Bill Murray is up to his old antics again. David Feherty, what's going on down there?"

Feherty, laughing, reports, "Well, Jimmy, Bill Murray just threw Madeleine Albright face-first into a sand trap, to the delight of the gallery here. At least I think it was delight. It's hard to tell with these North Koreans. They're not terribly emotive. The whole thing was a riot: it took both Dan Marino and Tom Bergeron to get Secretary Albright out of the hazard. She was in stitches. Classic Murray, guys."

Nantz and Faldo laugh back in the booth. As the camera cuts back to them too soon, viewers catch a half second of the government minders making throat-slash gestures to the announcing pair. Nantz and Faldo stop laughing immediately. Nantz continues.

"Inappropriate public conduct by Bill Murray there. Not funny at all." The government minders straighten back up.

"Nick, you were telling me in the prisoner transport vehicle on the way over to the course this morning that you've been particularly impressed with what you've seen out of Bill Clinton this week."

"I really have, Jimmy. President Clinton, a decent golfer for a man with his schedule, is clearly comfortable here in North Korea. Remember, he was invited to this country by the Dear Leader personally to rescue those two American journalists a while back, and he really appears to be in his element. The former president is playing in a group with the entire losing team from last year's Lingerie Bowl. Certainly a larger group than you'd typically see at a major golf event, slowing down play considerably, but he's striking the ball nicely."

Nantz jumps in. "Yes, President Clinton was telling me earlier today, 'What happens in Pyongyang stays in Pyongyang,' as he snapped on his lambskin golf glove. He also said something about 'hittin' 'em long and hard with his five-wood' as he gestured to his playing partners." Nantz realizes he has disclosed too much.

"But he does great charitable work around the world and whatnot. So, you know."

"Anyhoo, we're going to step away for a commercial here. If the break feels a little longer than usual, it's because Nick and I will be receiving our bihourly performance review from North Korean government officials. Please pray for us. Seriously. We send you to break with our current leaderboard here at the 7th Annual Kim Jong-il Celebrity Golf Challenge." Nantz looks at his notes one more time, takes a deep breath, and reads in a defeated monotone, "Also, America sucks big donkey balls. That's what it says on this card here: that America sucks, uh, sucks big donkey balls." The government minders chuckle behind Nantz as the leaderboard goes up.

7TH ANNUAL KIM JONG-IL CELEBRITY GOLF CHALLENGE

Democratic People's Golf and Racquet Club

Pyongyang, North Korea

LEADERS

KIM JONG-IL	-31
ALONZO MOURNING	-8
CRAIG T. NELSON	-8
KOFI ANNAN	-7
ELISABETH HASSELBECK	-7
KEVIN SORBO	-6
SUGAR RAY LEONARD	-5
HALEY JOEL OSMENT	-4
CHIPPER JONES	-4
LADY GAGA	-2

Notables: Robert Mugabe (E), Dennis Franz (+2), Darryl Strawberry (+12)

TRUE STORY . . .

ATTENTION, WALMART SLAPPERS
Stranger smacks crying two-year-old at Walmart

There are two immutable truths about kids: 1) other people's children are annoying, and 2) despite your disdain, you are not allowed to hit those other people's children. A 61-year-old man observed the first rule at the Walmart in Stone Mountain, Georgia, but broke the second, all-important one.

When a 2-year-old girl starting crying inside the store, the mean old bastard warned her mother that if she couldn't shut the child up, he'd be glad to help her. The crying continued, apparently interrupting the man's efforts to find a reasonably priced shower caddy or whatever it was that he needed to focus on. He approached the little girl and smacked her in the face several times. According to police, he then said, "See, I told you I would shut her up." Yes, he talked trash about smacking a 2-year-old.

Security subdued the man until local police arrived. The man was convicted of felony cruelty to a child. Of course, if the girl's father had been at the Walmart that day, there would have been a visitation and burial scheduled instead of a court hearing.

After serving his time, the Georgia man expressed remorse and promised to serve out the remainder of his days on this Earth not frightening children, but doing what he does best: stomping puppies.

15

The Neverland Ranch Yard Sale

★

OWN A PIECE OF HISTORY!
NEVERLAND RANCH YARD SALE
EVERYTHING MUST GO!!!

Hosted by Tito, Jermaine, Marlon, Randy,
Jackie, La Toya, and Rebbie* Jackson
With Special Performance by Janet Jackson

*Yes, she's one of the Jacksons. You can look it up on the Internet.

The sudden death of Michael Jackson in June 2009 set off a protracted family feud over his estate. After months of ugly negotiation, Jackson's eight siblings and their parents, Joe and Katherine, finally agreed that the only fair solution was to hold an old-fashioned yard sale at Michael's Neverland Ranch, with the proceeds split equally among them. Joe appointed himself to run the event, citing a reluctance to "trust the rest of y'all dumb motherfuckers."

Excerpts of the original minutes from the planning meeting for the yard sale were entered into evidence as part of a class-action fraud lawsuit brought by the Jackson children against Joe Jackson. Attorneys for the Jackson siblings argue that Joe embezzled money from the yard sale, whose proceeds were to be shared evenly. The plaintiffs say the meeting minutes are evidence of Mr. Jackson's strong-arming, humiliation, and early plans to cheat them out of their share of the profits. The portion of the document entered into evidence reads as follows:

JOE JACKSON arrives 45 minutes late.

JOE JACKSON immediately appoints himself manager and executive producer of the Neverland Ranch Yard Sale.

JOE JACKSON declares none of the proceeds from the sale will go to charity as previously proposed, saying, "That was some bullshit to make us look good in the press as we ghoulishly pick over the possessions of our dead son and brother."

JOE JACKSON tells La Toya to "shut up and lose 15 pounds." When there is absolute quiet, he goes around the conference table and hands out the following assignments with raised voice, beginning with Jermaine.

JERMAINE

Sell that goddamn roller coaster and the Ferris wheel from the backyard. These are our big-ticket items. Find one of those obsessed freaks who used to dress up like Michael with the glove and shit. Those people will do anything to get a piece of Michael. Or invite some rich asshole whose little brat daughter wants a roller coaster from Michael Jackson's house for her Sweet Sixteen. You've seen that shit on MTV where the man spends a million dollars on a birthday party for his ugly-ass daughter to make up for the fact that nobody likes her and boys won't go near her ugly ass. Find one of those suckers. There's also a steam locomotive and an entire railroad system back there, for fuck's sake. Get rid of all that shit. And scrub it down, too. I don't even want to think about what that skin-bleaching freak was doing on the kiddie coaster. Don't fuck this up like you have everything else in your wasted life, Jermaine. I can't believe I thought about making you the lead singer. Goddamn!

TITO

Get all that Peter Pan bullshit out my sight. Michael was the most talented, the most successful, and, of course, my favorite because of it, but goddamn he was one messed-up boy. Got pictures of a flying little boy in green tights all over his house. Think that might have set off some alarms when you're dropping your kid off at the ranch for the weekend, Mom? Goddamn. And sell those statues outside of children holding hands, singing songs, and doing jump rope and shit. Where do you even buy some shit like that? Makes me want to puke. Find some pervert who wants that shit. Oh, and Tito, it should have been you in that casket.

MARLON

Do something with that motherfuckin' zoo out there. Jesus Christ. Got llamas and alpacas wandering around the backyard, shitting all over the place. Who the fuck has a zoo in their yard? Sell those smelly-ass animals to a farm or a zoo or a fur coat company. Keep that ostrich though. I like that crazy motherfucker. And if you see Bubbles the Chimp back there, get that tuxedo he wore to the Grammys. That shit was expensive. Marlon, this is a chance to redeem yourself and bring back some of the money your lack of talent cost the band back in the day. We never would have broken up if you'd been better. Redeem your ass.

JACKIE

Which one are you again? Put on a clown costume and stand by the goddamn highway and wave people into the sale. Get some big-ass shoes and a funny wig and some colorful-as-hell balloons. Make some signs, too, and put them up around town. Make them say something like, HEY, COME TO NEVERLAND RANCH AND BUY SOME OF MICHAEL JACKSON'S FAMOUS SHIT! WE PROMISE NOBODY WILL TOUCH YOU! Come on, that shit is funny. Laugh. You're the marketing department, Jackie. If no one shows up to this yard sale, it's your fault. Try to make this your first personal success since you got me a beer out of the refrigerator in 1972.

LA TOYA

Set up a lemonade stand, baby. Make some cookies and some of those Rice Krispies Treats—and don't leave 'em in the oven for so goddamn long this time. They're supposed to be chewy, not like goddamn marshmallow-filled bricks. Sell some of that Jesus Juice from Michael's 3-acre underground wine cavern, too. That's the original shit. It's famous. People don't care that it was used to get 12-year-old boys drunk. They'd buy O.J.'s bloody gloves if they could. People are fucked up. Jack up the price on that shit, La Toya. And, by the way, you could have been Janet if you hadn't been so dumb, lazy, and overweight.

JANET

Put on a tight little outfit and dance in a cage while you sing your greatest hits. I don't want to hear any backtalk on that. And don't sleepwalk through the performance like you did at the opening of my Bentleys-only car wash in Encino. I'm recording this one and releasing it as *Janet Jackson: One Night Only. Live from the Yard Sale at Her Dead Brother's Weird-Ass Kiddie Ranch*. Also, go make me a sandwich. I know you don't think you're too big to make your daddy a sandwich. Remember, Janet: I brought you into this world and I'll take you out of this motherfucker right quick. Now go work on your choreography for the yard sale.

REBBIE

You're my firstborn and I love you like hell. Shit, you're almost as old as I am. Literally. But nobody knows who you are. You just aren't weird enough. I'd have you run the books for this yard sale, but I obviously plan on ripping all you dumb mother-fuckers off, so I can't have you stickin' your nose in the numbers. Shit, I don't know: just sit in a dunk tank and let motherfuckers knock your ass in the water for money. Shit will be funny as hell. Laugh. Either that or stay home. No one's gonna notice.

KATHERINE

You just sit there and don't say shit.

On the day of the sale, Joe Jackson's operation ran exactly as planned in that first meeting. He barked fatherly motivation as the Jackson boys peddled their brother's eccentric wares ("I will punch you in the mouth with a roll of quarters in my hand if you don't sell those goddamn bumper cars!" he'd say). La Toya sold lemonade, chewy Rice Krispies Treats, and copies of her 1985 fitness video *La Toning with La Toya* from a card table. Janet entertained shoppers, dancing in a cage that dangled from a crane and singing a medley from *Rhythm Nation 1814* for an upcoming live album whose profits would belong exclusively to Joe. Jackie, dressed in the oversize clown suit, sobbed loudly by the side of the road as he futilely waved cars into the sale. Katherine sat there and didn't say shit, as instructed.

The Neverland Yard Sale attracted an array of memorabilia collectors, exotic animal dealers, and Saudi oil sheiks. Curiosity seekers were discouraged, however, by the event's $1,000 cash cover charge and the large, handwritten sign that read, IF YOU'RE NOT BUYING SHIT, GET THE FUCK OUT!—THE MANAGEMENT.

Despite the exorbitant price tags, nearly all the items from Michael Jackson's former home were snapped up in short order. The only items that remained at the end of the day were Jackson's stash of *Kids Incorporated* videotapes and his scrapbook collection of pressed umbilical cords.

Joe Jackson's public claims of "disappointing sales" were contradicted wildly by the sales ledger itself, a fact that dealt a blow to his defense against the embezzlement charges. Also, eyewitnesses observed Mr. Jackson loading garbage bags full of cash into a van and later crashing the rented vehicle through Neverland's front gate while laughing maniacally and yelling, "I stole all the money!" That certainly will not help his case either.

The following highlights from the Neverland Ranch sales ledger suggest extraordinary profits, to which the Jackson siblings have staked their legal claim.

Item: Herd of African Plains Zebras
Sale Price: $250,000

Item: Shrunken Head of Hermann Göring
Sale Price: $450,000

Item: Shroud of Turin (original)
Sale Price: $56,000,000,000

Item: Large portrait of Emmanuel Lewis (oil on canvas)
Sale Price: $2,500

Item: Emmanuel Lewis
Sale Price: N/A (adoption)

Item: Michael Jackson's Original Nose (Condition: Fair)
Sale Price: $1,500,000

Item: 1994 "America's Hottest Webelos" Calendar
Sale Price: $31

Item: Stuffed Remains of Liberace (posed at piano
with candelabra)
Sale Price: $173,000

Item: Macaulay Culkin's *Dukes of Hazzard* Underoos (worn)
Sale Price: $150

Item: Four (4) Working Intercontinental Ballistic Missiles
Sale Price: $20,000,000

Item: The *Titanic* (ship salvaged and rebuilt completely to
original specs)
Sale Price: $800,000,000

Item: Charlie Chaplin's Testicles (pickled)
Sale Price: $21,000

18

Operation Pick 'n Pair: The Way Forward in Afghanistan

★

THE UNITED STATES OF AMERICA
DEPARTMENT OF DEFENSE

Mr. President,

At your request, we have prepared a list of alternative strategies for the way forward in Afghanistan. As you noted astutely in your letter to this department, our current war plan "blows."

We are as determined as you are, sir, to win the fight in Afghanistan and to bring our troops home as soon, and as honorably, as possible.

While I took your specific policy critique to heart, I would respectfully challenge your assertion, Mr. President, that the Defense Department has been "run like a Chuck E. Cheese" in recent years. We take our responsibility to defend this great country very seriously. We've just had a tough run here lately. We would ask you, sir, not to let a couple of dud wars overshadow all the hits we've had—the same way you give a pass to De Niro for *Meet the Fockers* and *Analyze That*. Those atrocities cannot tarnish the legacy of *Taxi Driver* and *Raging Bull*. Same thing here with Iraq and Afghanistan. We still defeated Hitler and the Japs. No one can take that away from us.

With that said, the United States Department of Defense humbly submits the following new war strategy proposals for your consideration. To be honest with you, Mr. President, we've already had thousands of ideas that haven't worked, so we're a little tapped out. This time we went outside the box, allowing our summer interns to pitch ideas in exchange for college credit. In short, we threw a bunch of shit against the wall. Let's see what sticks. It couldn't be any worse than what we're doing now, right?

Thank you as always for your input, sir.

Respectfully,
Robert M. Gates
United States Secretary of Defense

AFGHANISTAN: THE WAY FORWARD
PREPARED BY THE UNITED STATES
DEPARTMENT OF DEFENSE

Operation Pick 'n Pair

As DOD and POTUS have discussed on numerous occasions, a complete withdrawal from Afghanistan will be appropriate and justified as soon as the country resembles a civilized, governable, and even marginally developed Western country. Reasonable progress—real or perceived—will allow for a declaration of victory by the United States of America and its allies (but mostly by us).

With that in mind, DOD proposes the immediate groundbreaking for no fewer than one hundred (100) Applebee's Neighborhood Grill and Bar locations across Afghanistan. What says "unspoiled Americana" better than an Applebee's, for heaven's sake? We believe, sir, that images of everyday Afghanis enjoying two-for-one happy hour margaritas and the CNN pictures of parents taking their smiling children for a sensibly priced dinner of boneless Buffalo wings and wonton tacos will convince people back home that you have managed to turn the tide in the war. Our computer models show that the reaction of an average American citizen will be, "Hey, that looks like *our* Applebee's! They made Afghanistan all nice! Shit, I'm hungry." That citizen will then return to watching professional wrestling before ordering a pizza from Papa John's, leaving no need for empirical evidence of actual progress. The sale is made.

A sense of relief and national pride will wash over the American public when it appears victory is at hand in Afghanistan. Who could argue in good conscience that the United States has *not* won when you have insurgents laying down their arms and sharing a "Pick 'n Pair," where they can choose any combination of two of Applebee's Simmering Soups, Sensational Salads, sandwiches, or pasta—all for one low price? These Afghani insurgents will, of course, be played by actors currently living in Los Angeles. We already have a stack of headshots. This, sir, is your Hollywood ending to a long and costly war.

DOD would suggest that Vice President Biden appear for a ribbon-cutting ceremony at the flagship Applebee's restaurant in Kabul to drive home the impression that the rock-solid foundations for democracy and Western convenience have been laid in Afghanistan. They will not have been, of course, but that's hardly the point.

To bolster the case that sufficient progress has been made, we will build the façade of a strip mall around each of the Applebee's restaurants—kind of like you see in those old Westerns. Entire communities springing up overnight and made entirely out of plywood you can buy at Home Depot. We have approached the Hollywood production designer who did all the *Lord of the Rings* movies for an estimate. He's really quite good.

In summary, the epic failures of both the British and the Soviets in Afghanistan over the course of history have earned the country a reputation as "the Graveyard of Empires." With the construction of just a handful of Applebee's franchises, you, sir, could be the president to transform Afghanistan into "the Home of the Spicy Shrimp Diavolo!" The course of history would be changed forever. An Ann Taylor Loft store and an NBA franchise would not be far behind.

Operation "D-day: The Sequel!"

This one may strike you as counterintuitive, but hear us out: start another war. That's right, do something so preposterous that the American people forget about Afghanistan altogether. Trust me, they're just begging for a reason to forget about that shithole anyway. Please forgive the language, Mr. President, but it really is just about the worst place on the face of the Earth. It's like rural Nevada with 30-year-old land mines all over the place. Have you been? Just awful.

The Department of Defense has a proposal that will not only make the country forget about Afghanistan, but remember a simpler, happier time in our nation's history. We have a plan in place whereby the United States military would re-create the D-day landings on the beaches of Normandy, France. A full-scale reproduction of Operation Overlord as conducted on June 6, 1944, would divert the world's attention and strike a nostalgic chord at home. People love a sequel, Mr. President.

Picture heroic young men and women throwing open the doors of Higgins boats and storming the beaches as actors dressed as Nazis fire cap guns at them. Imagine American tanks rolling slowly through the streets of Bayeux as children throw chocolates and women in cotton dresses wave from doorways.

Think of servicemen from varied backgrounds (a streetwise New Yorker and a simple country boy from Georgia, for example) shacking up together in quaint French farmhouses to hide out from the enemy—*Saving Private Ryan* comes to life. BTW, can you believe that queer Shakespeare movie beat *Saving Private Ryan* for Best Picture that year?! What a crock of horseshit.

Here's the great news: most of the kids in the United States are so dumb, they think D-day actually *was* created by Steven Spielberg for a movie. And, with all due respect, a large portion of the Greatest Generation that lived through the real thing may not remember the day themselves at this point. As far as 90 percent of America is concerned, you, Mr. President, will have presided over one of the most important days in American history. The sins of Afghanistan will be forgotten and the spirits of a war-weary nation lifted when those servicemen and -women come home from Paris and parade through the Canyon of Heroes in New York City. Oh, and not that you're in this for personal reasons, but how did D-day work out for Eisenhower? National hero. Two-term president. Highway system named after him. Catch my drift?

You'll obviously have to make some kind of a diplomatic arrangement with the leadership in France before we launch "Operation D-day: The Sequel!"—maybe promise Sarkozy box seats to a Wizards game or something—but honestly that's not my problem.

Not to brag, but we thought this one was pretty goddamn

good. We came up with it while we were playing Call of Duty 2 on the giant monitor in the Situation Room. Badass, right?

Operation *Jersey Shore*

Mr. President, I mentioned earlier in this memo that, out of complete and utter desperation, we solicited ideas from our summer interns. We had a "What the Hell Should We Do in Afghanistan?" essay contest, with the winner getting a CIA tote bag, water bottle, and fanny pack. We thought, "Hey, we're all getting a little gray in the beard around here, why not tap into the ideas and energy of America's youth? Couldn't hurt, right?" Wrong.

Sir, I will not waste your time or insult the office of the president of the United States by sharing most of what these dipshits came up with, but I just had to share part of one proposal. The following is from a person educated in the American university system. We had to accept his application because his father secretly financed a covert operation we ran last year to try to overthrow the British monarchy (tell you about that one next time we catch up). Without further ado, Operation *Jersey Shore*, brought to you by the future of America. God help us.

You guyz should todes send the cast of *Jersey Shore* into Afghanistan. LMAO! First of all Situation, Ronnie, and Pauly D are super-jacked and eff'd so many people up in bar fights. Can you imagine what they'd do if you gave them guns?!

If you do this one, you should rip the sleeves off those camo jackets dudes wear over there to show juiced arms and Pauly's tats that are off the chain (Urban Outfitters has bangin' tank tops and sleeveless tees). You think bin Laden or whatever wants to see those boyz rollin' up on the set? Helllllllll no!!!!

Snooki and JWoWW are tough as shiznit, too, for chicks. I wouldn't want to fight those bitches if I was a dumb terrorist. Plus, they could like liberate the women in Afghanistan and show them how to lose the burkas or whatever and look HOT! Show some f'in cans and leg, for Allah's sake! Those Middle East chicks are kinda heinous (hahahaha)! Little tanning and hair spray could start a feminist revolution. For reals!

All kidding aside, the *Jersey Shore* crew is tough as hell and wouldn't take any shit from a bunch of people who smell like ass. We wear down the enemy Jersey-style and it's GAME OVER! You saw what happened to the last guy who stepped to them at a nightclub in Seaside and tried to steal their Jäger shots. Night, night—you're sleepin'! One shot, kid! No more pussyin' around like little bitches, Mr. Secretary. Send in the Situation!!!

Hey, are we getting reimbursed for meals and commute this summer? That shit adds up, man.

Peace,
Patrick "P-Diddy" Peterson
DOD Intern

Pompton Lakes, NJ
University of West Virginia, Class of ?? (we'll see!)

Mr. President, after a careful review, you'll be relieved to know that we have decided against sending the cast of MTV's *Jersey Shore* into Afghanistan. Say the word and we will a) invade France, or b) start hiring servers for the Kabul Applebee's. By the way, have you tried their Asiago Peppercorn Steak? Try it and thank me later. That's a direct order from the Secretary of Defense.☺

17

Levi Johnston: The College Essay

★

THE UNIVERSITY OF CALIFORNIA, BERKELEY

Application for Admission

PERSONAL INFORMATION

Name: LEVI K. JOHNSTON

DOB: 5/3/1990

Race: WHITE GUY

Hometown: WASILLA, ALASKA

High School: WASILLA H.S.—GO WARRIORS!

GPA: PRETTY GOOD

Academic Concentration: NOT SO GOOD (A.D.D.)

PERSONAL STATEMENT

Grades and scores tell only a small part of your story. Please use the space below to share with us some background or life experience that will make you a unique contributor to the forward-thinking social culture and strenuous academic environment at Berkeley. Keep in mind there are tens of thousands of people dying to get into our elite university at this very moment, so this had better be good. Seriously, don't waste our time. Also, we're extraordinarily, even heroically, open-minded at Berkeley about race, religious preference, and gender reassignment, so if you're just a regular white guy you've got your work cut out here. Good luck—especially to the vegan, Marxist, transgender Pacific Islanders.

Well, I don't know anything about Marxist trannies, but I promise I've got more life experience in my left ball than any of the other freaks you're looking at. Here's the deal: I've been doing the Hollywood thing for a couple years now—acting, modeling, a tiny bit of male exotic dancing, etc.—and I figure it's time to make people think I'm working on my smarts. My manager says the public sees me as a bit of a mumbling dumbass, so we figured going to a famous college full of nerds like yours is a good move for me. Kind of a James Franco/Natalie Portman thing. (He's talented *and* smart?! Damn!) Most of the nerd schools are on the East Coast and I sure as hell ain't moving that far from Wasilla. I'm also looking closely at Stanford. Tiger went there and he is THE MAN!

A lot of people seem to think my life started the day I knocked up Bristol Palin. Not true. I mean, the cool part started then, but there was some other stuff before that. I grew up in Wasilla, Alaska, a town with like 10,000 people outside Anchorage. Our old mayor was a woman named Sarah Palin. Maybe you've heard of her. That was back when Sarah was cool as shit before her head got all big from being governor and almost vice president of America. BTW, I can't believe I'm going back to Palinworld with this whole marriage deal Awkward!

Now I know your whole thing is academics and libraries and experiments and pencils and all, but I'll just be honest: the books have never been my strong suit. Hockey and huntin' were my thing. Still are. I'm pretty damn good at both, if you want to know the truth. I hope like hell there's somewhere to hunt caribou in Berkeley. They only shoot *people* down here in L.A. What's the fun in that?

I want you to know that despite getting a late start, I've really taken to reading in recent months. I check out the "Just Like Us" section of *Us Weekly* all the time. Did you know Nicole Kidman buys her produce at the farmers' market right across the street from the GNC where I get my protein powder? Crazy, right? I don't want to lay on the literary credentials too thick, but I'm penning the foreword for the upcoming unauthorized biography of Spencer Pratt written by the editorial board of *Star* magazine.

But you're not looking at me for my reading and writing skills—you've got plenty of superdorks covering you in that department. You want me around because I'm a celebrity. You want me at Cal because I can bring a little cool to your hippy nerd factory. So let me just lay out the "life experiences" you say you're looking for. The same life experiences, by the way, that made me #11 on Salon.com's 2009 Sexiest Man Living list (you can look it up on Google or Ask Jeeves.com).

For starters I've got this cool little boy named Tripp. I made him with

Sarah's daughter Bristol. You've probably read about that part on Gawker. By the way, contrary to those "deadbeat dad" reports, I Skyped with that kid all the time. So I don't want to hear any of this shit about me neglecting my kid while I posed for nudie magazines in L.A. Skype is like being in the same room as your son except he's inside a computer.

Anyway, Sarah was all uptight about Bristol being pregnant because she was running for vice president with that weird old guy McCain, so we went public with it. Some New York–sounding lady called the house in Wasilla and said, "Don't talk to the press. We'll have you out of that shitty town and into some real clothes within the hour." That wasn't very cool, but I just did what they said cuz honestly I didn't have shit else to do. They bought me a faggy suit and put me on a plane to Minnesota or Wisconsin or Nebraska or something. On the plane, a scary-looking woman told me real simple, "Don't open your fucking mouth. Ever. You got that, you dumb hick?" I told her, "Yes, ma'am," and our journey began.

The McCain guy, who smells like a musty old shed covered in Aqua Velva, pulled me aside when I got to the Republican Convention in Milwaukee (or Michigan?). I'll never forget what he said. He said, "Son, if you fuck this up for me, I will rip off your head and shit down your neck! Don't test me because I will do it." Talk about life experience! The almost-president of America says he's going to take a dump down my neck after he rips off my melon! I tried real hard to remember that one.

So after the convention, we got on a plane and flew all over the goddamn place. For about a month and a half of my life there, I honestly had no idea what was going on. The campaign people got me a ball of yarn to play with so I wouldn't get bored as shit all the time. I just stood onstage in city after city with Sarah, Todd, Bristol, and the mean old guy and tried to stay awake by counting the MILFs in the crowd (FYI, Akron, Ohio, is full of 'em). There

Checkout Receipt

Santa Fe Springs City Library
1/19/11 11:13AM
Below is a list of items checked out:

Rance, Ronald Perry

American freak show : the completely fab
1284002618372 Due: 02/09/11

The black hand : the bloody rise and red
1284002752627 Due: 02/09/11

TOTAL: 2
PLEASE RETAIN THIS RECEIPT. IMPORTANT
DUE DATE AND FINE INFORMATION.
TO RENEW MATERIALS CALL 869-5723.

Thank You!

was lots of talking and waving and none of it did any good because Sarah and the mean, smelly old guy lost the election. The minute the race was over, a couple ladies took all the clothes from my hotel room while I was in the shower and left a $50 Greyhound Bus gift certificate on top of the TV set. The way I saw it, I had $50 in bus credit that I didn't have a minute before and Sarah's stupid vice president thing was finally over. Time to go home!

Back in Wasilla, Bristol and I got fake "engaged" for a while. Then we broke it off cuz tons of random hot girls started texting me and friending me on Facebook after the campaign, so I couldn't be tied down anymore. It got me away from the crazy Sarah lady, but the only thing was that I was stuck with a "Bristol" tattoo around my ring finger. The stupid things teenagers do when they're huffing paint, right? I spent a while trying to find another girl named Bristol to make the tattoo work, but that's not as easy as it sounds. I found one chick named Cristal, but that just turned out to be her stage name. Her real name was Aqualita. The tattoo guy said he couldn't rework "Bristol" into "Aqualita" so we split up. We still talk sometimes.

Once I unloaded the Bristol baggage, my shit really started to blow up. My manager (who is also a private investigator in Alaska—seriously) suggested I call myself Ricky Hollywood. I still don't really get it, but hey, man, the alter-ego thing worked for Garth Brooks (hello, Chris Gaines!), so why not Levi Johnston?

I did big TV interviews with Tyra Banks (even hotter in person) and Larry King (even more haunting in person). I went to the Teen Choice Awards with firecrotch Kathy Griffin (yes, boys, carpet = curtains). I wrote this big long story for *Vanity Fair* where I trashed Sarah real good. I didn't write it actually, but some writer dude did and I read it and was like, "Hell yeah!"

A bunch of people even said I was some kind of icon for fags after I posed nude in *Playgirl*. Sarah told Oprah later that I was doing "porn." That really frosted my balls. *Playgirl* is not porn. *Playgirl* is artistic and full of current events analysis that spits in the face of conventional wisdom. *Just Us Guys* and *Butt* magazines are porn. *Playgirl* is art. On the acting front, I did a random commercial for some pistachio company where I made fun of the fact that I'd knocked up my teenage girlfriend. Priceless! I was on top of the entertainment world.

Admittedly, things have tapered off lately in my acting/modeling/ appearing-at-bowling-alley-office-parties-for-money career. That's why I'm trying to lay low at your dork-a-palooza college for a few years. If you've got another applicant who became internationally famous for knocking up the daughter of a vice presidential candidate, I'd like to meet him. You asked for life experience and I just gave it to you. Bam! Do the right thing, Berkeley. Math nerds are a dime a dozen. There's only one Ricky Hollywood.

p.s.—You said applicants could include a family photo. As you can tell from my essay, my family is totally f**ked up, so instead please find attached a tasteful, full-length outtake from my *Playgirl* photo shoot. I dare you not to admit that, Cal.

REFERENCES

1. Brian "Pucks" Malone
JV hockey coach, Wasilla High School

2. "Big Brick"
Bouncer at Fubar in West Hollywood

3. Todd Palin

Baby mama's dad (we're still cool)

4. "Corey"

Photographer's assistant, *Playgirl* magazine

5. Jack Mehoff

(Just a funny-as-shit name)

TRUE STORY . . .

IS THAT A SONGBIRD IN YOUR PANTS?
Man arrested at LAX for smuggling rare birds

Add songbirds to the long list of items you apparently can't bring on a plane in our post-9/11 world. A 46-year-old man named Sony Dong was arrested at Los Angeles International Airport with 14 Vietnamese songbirds strapped to his legs and ankles. A heads-up U.S. Fish and Wildlife inspector became suspicious of Dong when he saw bird droppings on the passenger's shoes and feathers sticking out of the bottom of his pants. Dong copped to illegally importing wildlife after revealing that his pants were, indeed, stuffed with exotic birds.

Dong smuggled the rare songbirds from Vietnam to the United States, where he expected to fetch some $400 for each of them. One assumes Sony Dong planned to use the money to finance his fledgling Southeast Asian porn production outfit, Dong Enterprises.

18

The People of Heaven v. John Edwards

★

THE PEOPLE OF HEAVEN V. JOHN EDWARDS

CASE # 351-CR-8253

<u>TRANSCRIPT OF PROCEEDINGS</u>

BEFORE: THE HONORABLE SAINT PETER

DATE: October 12, 2041

PLACE: Courtroom #17-B

Pearly Gates, Heaven

ST. PETER: Good morning, Mr. Edwards. My time is short. I've got a backlog of purgatory cases to get through today, so let's begin. You are here without counsel?

MR. JOHN R. EDWARDS: I will be representing myself in this matter, St. Peter. As you may know, I was a wildly successful personal injury attorney in North Carolina for some time. Some have called me the finest trial lawyer in the history of—

ST. PETER: You were an ambulance chaser.

MR. EDWARDS: We prefer to think of ourselves as victims' advocates.

ST. PETER: Right. And you are here today because you want to get into Heaven? Seriously, man?

MR. EDWARDS: I am, St. Peter. I understand you are a jury of one and I respect the system you have in place here in Heaven. I do have concerns that your judgment may have been tainted by unfavorable, and unfair, media coverage of my life.

ST. PETER: Look, I've been doing this for a long time. Nobody gets through those gates behind me without getting the OK from St. Pete. I'm like a bouncer at a crazy-exclusive night-club, except if I let you in, you find eternal life instead of

$250 bottles of cheap vodka and skanks dancing on tables. I take my responsibility very seriously and I never prejudge, but I do have cable TV and WiFi up here. Based on what I've seen—and maybe I shouldn't say this, but here goes—you seem like a bit of an evil, phony douche. But again, I'm a fair arbiter and I will base your admission into—or rejection from—Heaven on the facts and only the facts. The burden of proof rests upon you, Mr. Edwards. I am ready to hear your case.

MR. EDWARDS: I appreciate your objectivity, St. Peter. I'd like to begin by—

ST. PETER: I mean, I just have to say though, and then I'll let you start, that thing with the kooky mistress chick was messed up, man. I'm pretty jaded—I've seen a lot up here over the last couple thousand years—but I read that one and I was like, "Daaaaammmnnnn!" It just kept getting worse, you know?

MR. EDWARDS: I'm not proud of that part of my life, St. Peter, but it was a long time ago and I would hope you wouldn't let that terrible episode overshadow the good works I did during my time on Earth. For example, I once got a client an award of $7 million from the North Carolina Department of Transportation after he picked up and brutally murdered a drifter.

ST. PETER: Jesus Christ, man. What the . . .

MR. EDWARDS: That hitchhiker should never have been allowed to walk anywhere near the highway. That was a preventable premeditated murder. Shame on the highway department for putting my client in a position where he had to pick up and murder that man. That's just one of many cases of my helping those victims who cannot help them- selves. Just the way you and Jesus used to do it. So if I could just proceed—

ST. PETER: I'm just gonna pretend I didn't hear that crazy- ass shit from a guy trying to get into Heaven. Now, I swear I'll let you have the floor after this, but I want to get this into the record clearly before we move on: you cheated on your cancer-stricken wife with some nutcase broad who—and I honestly hate to say this because I'm not like this—wasn't even that hot?

MR. EDWARDS: Well, that's certainly a matter of opinion, St. Peter. She was interesting-looking. And she challenged me. Our energies matched. I learned from her. For example, did you know that Gandhi and John Lennon were both Libras? Explains a lot, doesn't it?

ST. PETER: No, it doesn't. So you've got this crazy chick and you figure the smart move is to hire her and let her follow you around with a video camera! A video camera! I've got an idea, crazy New Age stalker lady: let's make sure we document this affair . . . during a presidential campaign! Wow! I can't decide if you're ballsy or just dumb as shit. Either way, thank God you weren't president, right? Jesus, Mary, and Joseph!

MR. EDWARDS: Again, mistakes were made. I'd like to move past that part of—

ST. PETER: But wait, it gets better—and this is my last interruption, you have my word. You knock up the moony mistress, tell the world the baby isn't yours, and then ask the campaign guy who picks up your dry cleaning and wipes your ass to say the kid is his?! Seriously, dude, where do you get the sack to even think of something like that? I'm actually impressed in a weird way.

MR. EDWARDS: I admitted to poor judgment at the time. I was eventually very candid about my transgressions. And, for the record, I wiped my own behind almost always during my time on Earth. I'm not sure I like the path we're heading down here. May I proceed?

ST. PETER: Look, Mr. Edwards, I don't mean to bust your balls, but you have to admit you've got a pretty tough case to make here today.

MR. EDWARDS: And I intend to make it, St. Peter.

ST. PETER: I get it, bro. Life throws you curveballs. Hell, I was just a fisherman who fell in with the right crowd in Galilee. I'm under no illusions. If I hadn't met J.C., I probably would have ended up working an overnight shift warming up combo baskets at the 24-hour Long John Silver's up here when it was all said and done. But, as luck would have it, Jesus and I hit it off famously at the dog run one day after my little Yorkie ran off with one of His sandals. Long story short, we became boys, and here I am with the keys to the Kingdom of Heaven. That's not to say I didn't earn them, of course. Running around spreading the good news for J.C. wasn't all the Bible has cracked it up to be. The hours were a bitch. The pay was all this bogus deferred "eternal happiness" crap. And it took months to get reimbursed on expense reports.

MR. EDWARDS: What?

ST. PETER: I'm sorry, you don't want to hear all this. That's just life on the campaign trail, right? Spreading the Gospel. Of course, you were spreading some bullshit about "Two Americas" and I was spreading, let's see what was it again, oh yeah . . . Christianity! Anyway, I'm getting off on a tangent here. What I'm saying is we can't control the circumstances of our lives. God put Jesus in my life. He put that broken-down wackjob Rielle in yours.

I hope you don't mind if I give my opinion on that. What do

I know about women, right? I spent my life wandering
around with a pack of men in open-toed shoes.

MR. EDWARDS: It's your court, St. Peter, but I think she
was, in many ways, a beautiful woman. Her heart was made
of gold. Perhaps the problem is that your potential remains
blocked by negative energy. Do you practice New Age mysti-
cism? I could get you a brochure.

ST. PETER: No, I'm good. I'm just surprised you took the bait
from a broad who had "crazy" written across her forehead.
Maybe you were too busy reading each other's Tarot cards to
notice.

MR. EDWARDS: I appreciate your point of view. If I could
take it all back, I certainly would consider doing so. Truly.
May I?

ST. PETER: I apologize. I'll shut up now. Proceed with your
case.

MR. EDWARDS: Thank you. St. Peter, I'm the son of a mill
worker. When I say that, I do so because I hope it somehow
will cause you to view me in a more sympathetic light. The
"son of a mill worker" thing means my parents had a strong
work ethic and implies that, maybe by association, I do too.
It means I haven't always lived in a giant compound with a

movie theater and an indoor squash court. It means I'm not just a stuffed suit with great hair. Not that it's going to make a difference here, but the hair really is great. It has a combination of body and sheen that you rarely find in men.

ST. PETER: I can see that, Mr. Edwards. It's remarkable. It's clear you've treated it with great care.

MR. EDWARDS: Thank you, St. Peter. You know, the giant, almost obscene house and the perfect hair are all well and good, but it's important to know that I'm a man with a strong appreciation for what the good Lord has given him. Again, my father was a mill worker, so I would appreciate what I have now based on what he did not have. Does that make sense? I guess that display of humility I just showed is the mill worker in me. Like my dad. He worked in a mill of some sort.

ST. PETER: I understand.

MR. EDWARDS: Like an old-fashioned mill where people made things with their hands. They wore work clothes, perhaps overalls. I have to imagine they would have eaten their lunches from metal pails and waited for some sort of a bell or a whistle to call them back inside to continue making whatever it was they were making by hand. I'm sure there were injuries in these old mills—the kind that probably entitled the victims to millions in compensation from greedy, negligent corporations.

You see, I am related by blood to a person who did these things. I am the son of a mill worker. I would never put myself in your sandals, St. Peter, or tell you how to do your job, but from where I'm sitting, being the son of someone who was in the working class oughta be worth something up here.

ST. PETER: For one thing, Mr. Edwards, we don't admit people into Heaven on the basis of nepotism. We judge the life of the individual on its own merits. I want to be very clear on that. I make no exceptions. Just ask Nancy Sinatra.

More important, your father e-mailed my office and asked, as a personal favor, that we deny your application. He wrote, and I quote, "Put John on the elevator to the bottom floor, if you know what I mean."

MR. EDWARDS: Daddy said that?

ST. PETER: He sure did. It's harsh, I know.

MR. EDWARDS: Well, he's a loser anyway. F**kin' guy worked in a textile mill his whole life. No ambition. Pathetic. You can tell him I said that, too.

ST. PETER: Oh, dear. Mr. Edwards, you may proceed, but I have to tell you this is like watching a man drown slowly. I have that conflicted feeling when someone is struggling in the water right in front of you: Do I play the hero or do I keep these chinos dry and hope someone else dives in? Don't put me in that position, man. They don't pay me to hand out legal advice around here, but I'd get off the "son of a mill worker" thing.

MR. EDWARDS: Very well, St. Peter. I'm sure your heart broke the way mine did when you watched the aftermath of Hurricane Katrina. It was bad for obvious death and traffic reasons, but good because it allowed me to resurrect a slogan I coined that everyone had previously ignored—the one you were kind enough to shout out a moment ago: "Two Americas."

ST. PETER: That was not a shout-out.

MR. EDWARDS: Well, thanks just the same. To give you an idea of how concerned I was about the "Two Americas," I launched my presidential campaign in New Orleans in the part where all the poor people live. Do you know that not one of the homes in the 9th Ward has a billiards room with vintage movie posters and pinball machines? Not a single one. It breaks your heart.

To show my compassion, I wore a pair of jeans and a button-down shirt with the sleeves rolled up on that first day (it was back to the Armani suits with the tags cut out after that, of course). The jeans and rolled-up sleeves were to let America know that I was willing to get my hands dirty and be around poor people. Don't tell me Jesus wouldn't have loved that. That guy lived for the poor people photo-op.

ST. PETER: Honestly, I'm not even going to tell Jesus you were here.

MR. EDWARDS: I was very concerned about the "Two Americas," St. Peter. I even had a bunch of folks from America #2 pour the concrete for my wine cellar. That's not just talking about the "Two Americas." That's doing something about it.

ST. PETER: Your defense has gotten so bad it's almost good now.

MR. EDWARDS: Thank you, St. Peter.

ST. PETER: Hey, let's talk more about that weirdo chick you were banging.

MR. EDWARDS: Really? I'd rather not.

ST. PETER: Just out of curiosity, what was the plan if you won the presidential nomination that year? Or if, God forbid, you became president? Just move the baby mama into the Lincoln Bedroom? Bring her to the state dinners?

MR. EDWARDS: Again, St. Peter, I have said repeatedly that I am sorry for my behavior at that time. With due respect, I'm a little frustrated by the line of questioning here today. My assistant back on Earth was told that if I said I had allowed Christ into my heart, he would kind of assume the guilt for the sins and we could fast-track this process. My name should be on the list. Is there something that can be arranged?

ST. PETER: No, Mr. Edwards. There definitely is nothing to be arranged.

MR. EDWARDS: I would like to request a change of venue. The court clearly has been biased by media coverage and by the facts of my life.

ST. PETER: There are no other venues, Mr. Edwards. This is the Supreme Court to end all Supreme Courts. The end of the line. Do you have any closing remarks or should I just pull the trap door and send you downstairs now?

MR. EDWARDS: St. Peter, from my hardscrabble upbringing as the son of a mill worker I rose to a position where I actually had a working textile mill on the grounds of my property. My clothes were handmade on the premises. I would often visit the factory floor to check on the progress of a cardigan sweater or a blazer and think of my father, the mill worker. So it is with great humility that I ask you—

ST. PETER: I can't listen to this shit anymore. I hope those mill workers made you some lightweight linen slacks, Mr. Edwards. It gets warm where you're going.

Your application is denied. This one wasn't even close. Bailiff, see Mr. Edwards to the elevator.

MR. EDWARDS: Wait! There are "Two Americas"! Get your hands off me! Mill workers! My dear wife! Mystical powers! You can't do this to me! Don't you know who I am?!

ST. PETER: Laverne, I'm going to lunch. And tell Jesus I'm not gonna make it to racquetball this afternoon. Just make something up.

19

Snooki and the Salahis: The 15 Minutes Hall of Fame

★

A TRANSCRIPT of the remarks made by Master of Ceremonies Kevin Federline at the induction ceremony for the 15 Minutes Hall of Fame, Class of 2010.

G ood evening and welcome to El Segundo, California, home of the 15 Minutes Hall of Fame. Please continue to enjoy your lunch as we begin this afternoon's Fourteenth Annual Induction Ceremony. We have a great class to announce this year. As a 2005 inductee (*PAUSE FOR APPLAUSE*), I know how anxious our nominees are, so I'll unveil the list in just a moment—I promise, guys. Before I do, though, a word about the 15 Minutes Hall of Fame and the people who make it the world's largest and most highly regarded organization honoring the momentarily famous.

When Kato Kaelin founded this wonderful place in 1996 and made himself the charter member, it was little more than a small office space in an industrial park by the airport. Skeptics said Kato rented the place only so he could have somewhere to sleep and bathe himself. Well, that may have turned out to be true, but just look at us now. Kato, stand and be recognized, if you would. (*PAUSE FOR APPLAUSE*)

We have enshrined 120 distinguished members over the last thirteen years. Somewhere along the way we became the standard of excellence for former reality television stars and circus freak newsmakers. Only the very best of the best pass through those doors back there. Actually, the guys who rent the other half of the space for their counterfeit phone card business pass through the doors every morning, too, but you see what I'm driving at.

We are so honored to have some of the all-time greats with us this afternoon to help welcome our new class. Let's take a moment to say hello to them. To the radio contest winners here in attendance, please hold your applause until we have read the name of the last 15 Minutes Hall of Famer. The meet-and-greet with Larry Birkhead begins 15 minutes after our program here has concluded. Thank you.

First, from the Class of 1998, Miss Paula Jones. Paula reminds us that sometimes a brief brush with fame in an Arkansas hotel room is all it takes to become a household name. Welcome back, Paula.

Leading our Class of '99, in more ways than one, Mary Kay Letourneau, the middle school teacher who banged her

13-year-old student and later left her husband and four children for him. Nice to see you again, Mary Kay.

It's great to see Elián González back from our Class of 2000. Elián was the kid at the center of a story whose details I can't even remember. He wanted to go to Cuba, or he didn't want to go to Cuba? Who knows. It seems so quaint now. Pleasure to have you back with us, Gonzo.

Elián's classmate from that year is here as well: Darva Conger, stand up if you would. Reality TV was just a budding flower when you married and divorced that dude on *Who Wants to Marry a Multi-Millionaire?* back in 2000. Ladies and gentlemen, Darva was there for the infancy of reality television. A lot of people in this room owe her a great debt of gratitude. I probably shouldn't compare her to Rosa Parks, but I guess I just did. By the way, we invited Rosa to be an honorary member of the 15 Minutes Hall of Fame back in 1998, but she declined. Couldn't have been nicer about it. Anyway, welcome, Darva.

Is William Hung here? Bill, where are you? There you are, you old so-and-so. William was inducted in 2004. He pioneered the "sympathy celebrity" category. People simply felt bad about themselves for making fun of him on *American Idol* because, frankly, it looked like something might be wrong there. No one was making fun anymore when William released his Christmas album *Hung for the Holidays*. Had a heck of a run. He really is a strange duck though. Good to see you, Bill.

Couple folks to say hello to from the Class of 2005: Ken Jennings, of *Jeopardy!* fame, and Miss Jennifer Wilbanks, known to the world as the Runaway Bride. One's the kind of guy you want to have with you at trivia night down at the local sports bar. The other is the kind of gal who fakes her own kidnapping to get out of her wedding. He's a crazy genius. She's just plain old crazy. Have you seen those eyes? Yikes. Welcome back, Kenny and Jenny.

And, finally, a salute to our most recent inductee. From the Class of 2009, Joe the Plumber. One of the all-time greats to join this body. Who else can snake out your toilet by day and influence presidential politics by night? Joe, you were a terrific ambassador to the 15 Minutes Hall of Fame over the last year, representing our ideals of opportunism and desperation at every turn. We appreciate your service—and the free caulking in the men's room. Ladies and gentlemen, our returning 15 Minutes Hall of Famers. (*PAUSE FOR APPLAUSE*)

Now, if we could take the lights down, we will turn our attention to the men and women in this room hoping to join the rarefied space inhabited only by the likes of those men and women you just saw—American icons all. The lives of the four inductees whose names I will reveal in a moment are about to be changed forever. You, ladies and/or gentlemen, will join a club whose membership offers much, but demands even more. From this day forward, a prefix, and a burden of responsibility, will be attached to your name. You will be . . . a 15 Minutes Hall of Famer. (*PAUSE FOR APPLAUSE*)

Before we announce the new members, let's remind the audience of our nominees for the 15 Minutes Hall of Fame, Class of 2010.

She defines the kind of memorable reality TV character ripe for 15 minutes of fame—at once repellent and compelling. She also happens to be orange. Ladies and gentlemen, Nicole Polizzi, known to the world as Snooki from MTV's *Jersey Shore.* (★PAUSE FOR APPLAUSE★)

Our next nominee achieved stardom with the home-cooked recipe of a racy MySpace page, a catchy fake name, and a pinch of slutty bisexuality. She is the star of the reality show *A Shot at Love with Tila Tequila,* Miss Tila Tequila. (★PAUSE FOR AP-PLAUSE★)

His parents told the world he had floated away from their backyard in a homemade weather balloon. The police, and the national media, gave chase while he hid safely in a cardboard box in the attic at home. Please say hello to "Balloon Boy" Falcon Heene, and his creepy father, Richard. (★PAUSE FOR APPLAUSE★)

Our next nominee allowed the governor of New York to do things to her you wouldn't allow barnyard animals to do to each other. Her revelations about Client 9 took down an administration and gave the grateful state of New York a man named David Paterson. Ladies and gentlemen, Ashley Dupré. (★PAUSE FOR APPLAUSE★)

You know, it's one thing to alter your physical appearance to resemble your celebrity hero. It's quite another to have 14 children in that effort. A warm welcome for the pauper's Angelina Jolie, the Octomom, Miss Nadya Suleman. (★PAUSE FOR APPLAUSE★)

I'm not even sure our next nominee lasted 15 minutes, but he touched America—literally, in many cases—with his tickling, groping, snorkeling, and, yes, those famous "Massa Massages." He is former New York congressman, and current doughy, sweaty collector of porcelain figurines, Eric Massa. (★PAUSE FOR APPLAUSE★)

Up next, her older sister has become an international sex symbol. She has become the younger sister of an international sex symbol. Her highly publicized quickie marriage to a Los Angeles Laker was a bold, impressive attempt to grab attention away from her super-hot, bubble-assed sister Kim. Please welcome Khloe Kardashian. (★PAUSE FOR APPLAUSE★)

Our next nominee captured hearts around the world by reminding us that even homely looking people oughta have a fighting chance at fame. We're not usually big on internal beauty, but how about a nice round of applause for Susan Boyle, just the same. Let's hear it, folks. (★PAUSE FOR APPLAUSE/SYMPATHETIC STANDING OVATION BECAUSE SHE'S UGLY★)

Well, this beauty lectured us about the dangers of same-sex marriage while wearing a bikini and high heels on national television. She believes gay people are going to Hell, but we think she's a little slice of Heaven. Ladies and gentlemen, the former Miss California, Carrie Prejean. (★PAUSE FOR APPLAUSE★)

And our final nominees pushed their way into the White House, and in the process opened the door to fleeting fame. Might I say, they looked pretty darn good doing it, too. Whether they are inducted tonight or not, Tareq and Michaele Salahi have our respect for getting past the Secret Service to party with the president of the United States. Well done, you two.

Ladies and gentlemen, I give you the 2010 nominees for the 15 Minutes Hall of Fame. Good luck, all. (*PAUSE FOR APPLAUSE*)

One housekeeping note before we announce this year's inductees: Captain Chesley Sullenberger was nominated for a second consecutive year, but in a harshly worded e-mail, he declined our invitation to appear today. His message reads in part, "Ask the 155 people whose lives I saved by landing a jetliner with no engines on a river in New York City if I'm a 15-minute flash in the pan. You D-list frauds couldn't afford my appearance fee anyway. Lose the number. Sully out." His name has been removed from our nomination list permanently. He's not the man we thought he was. (*PAUSE FOR POSSIBLE APPLAUSE*)

All right, we've made them wait long enough. Let's meet the new members of the 15 Minutes Hall of Fame. If your name is not called, please remember that this is by no means the end of the road. A new reality show on VH1 or a nonviolent arrest could have you right back in this room next year. You all have an awful lot to be proud of.

Okay, here we go. (*PAUSE FOR EFFECT*) Why am I nervous? I'm just reading names. (*PAUSE FOR TENSION-BREAKING LAUGHTER*)

The first inductee in the Class of 2010 is . . . the Octomom! For the blatant exploitation of your 14 children just to appear in *Us Weekly* a few times, your name will join the list of 120 other Hall of Famers up on the Jessica Hahn Wall of Champions. Congratulations. Please come forward to receive your official 15 Minutes Hall of Fame digital watch by Casio and a gift certificate for a free order of garlic knots from our longtime sponsor Ray's Airport Pizza Hub.

The next member of the Class of 2010 is . . . I guess I should say "members," plural: the White House crashers, Tareq and Michaele Salahi! Richly deserved. You turned a party crash into a debate over national security. Come to think of it, did anybody invite you here tonight?! (*PAUSE FOR LAUGHTER FOR TOPICAL HUMOR*) Congratulations, you aren't just pathetic Washington social climbers anymore. You're Hall of Famers.

Boy, this is getting tense. So many worthy nominees still sitting there waiting to hear their names called. Let's see who's next.

The 15 Minutes Hall of Fame is proud to welcome . . . Snooki! Wow! I have to say, that's a bit of a surprise. Come on up here, you stumpy little tramp. Perhaps you were inducted because your fame so perfectly embodies the 15 Minutes spirit and reminds the world of America's coming collapse as a world power. Congratulations. Boy, forgive me for saying so, but you're gross in person.

Okay, we have just one more name to add to the Class of 2010. Again, if your name is not called, please remain calm and DO NOT attempt to flip over your table. They have been steel-bolted to the floor this year. I need not remind you of the Buster Douglas incident at last year's ceremony. That kind of behavior will not be tolerated and will lead to the automatic removal of your name from future consideration for admittance into the 15 Minutes Hall of Fame. There is quite simply no place in this hallowed, shared industrial park office space for that kind of shameless, self-serving conduct. (*PAUSE WITH SERIOUS FACE*)

Okay, here goes. Wow, they don't prepare you for the pressure. It just got so quiet in here. All right, deep breath. The final member of the 15 Minutes Hall of Fame Class of 2010 is . . . I knew it! Balloon Boy! Falcon Heene and his father, Richard! You went to unprecedented lengths to get your 15 minutes. Mr. Heene, you hid your 6-year-old son in the attic and temporarily convinced the world that he was hurtling toward his death in a UFO you built in your backyard. Again, you pretended your young son was dead so you could get a reality show. I think I speak for this entire body when I say we have scarcely seen a more worthy candidate for the 15 Minutes Hall of Fame. You are a sick, pathetic bastard—and we love you for it! Congratulations, Balloon Boy and Balloon Boy's crazy-ass dad.

Ladies and gentlemen, I give you the Class of 2010: The Octomom, the Salahis, Snooki, and Balloon Boy! What a group. (*PAUSE FOR BIG APPLAUSE*)

Thank you all for being here on this historic afternoon. I'm your host Kevin Federline, reminding you of the 15 Minutes Hall of Fame motto: "It doesn't matter why you're famous—as long as you are!"

INDEX*

*of the people I wish were in this book, but are not